Photo CD:

Quality Photos at Your Fingertips

John Larish

Micro Publishing Press
Torrance, California

Photo CD

Quality Photos at Your Fingertips

John Larish

Photo CD: Quality Photos at Your Fingertips
John Larish

Published by:
Micro Publishing Press
21150 Hawthorne Blvd., Suite 104
Torrance, CA 90503
(310) 371-5787

Copyright © 1993 by John Larish

First Printing, January, 1993

Printed in the United States of America

ISBN 0-941845-09-5

This book was imaged at RPI, Culver City, CA and printed at Delta Litho, Valencia, CA.

Dedicated to the men and women of Kodak whose vision of tomorrow's world of conventional photography and evolving digital imaging technology brought the Photo CD from concept to reality.

CONTENTS

Foreword ix

Introduction xi

Acknowledgments xv

Chapter 1: The New Era of Photography 1
What Is Photo CD? 5
Capabilities of Photo CD 7
Potential for Photo CD 10
Markets for Photo CD 16
Application Ideas for Photo CD 17
Bridge to the Future 20

Chapter 2: How Photo CD Works 21
Photo CD Disc Formats 23
Photo CD Master Image Format 25
How Photos CDs Are Mastered 29
Television Display 30
Professional Use of Photo CD 33
Using Photo CDs With a Computer 37
Photo CD Image Compression 41
Sound on a Photo CD Disc 42
Photo CD Access Developer Toolkit 44
Photo Industry Support of Photo CD 45
How Photo CDs Are Manufactured 46

Chapter 3: Printing Photo CD Images 49
Color Management of Digital Images 52
Prints from Photo CD 57
Large-Format Printing 68

Chapter 4: Enhancing Photo CD Images 71
Kodak Software 73
Software for Image Enhancement 78
Software For Color Control 91
Image Enhancement Workstations 92

Chapter 5: Publishing With Photo CD 95

Photo CD Catalog 97
Photo CD Portfolio 99
Conventional Publishing and Photo CDs 101
Standards in Prepress 104
Software For Publishing 107
Getting the Right Image for Publishing 113

Chapter 6: Legal Implications of Photo CD 117

Image Ownership and Rights 118
Legal Pitfalls 122
Clip-Art Photographs 125
The Legal Outlook 126

Chapter 7: The Compact Disc Family 131

Compact Disc Standards 132
Photo CD as an Archive Medium 138
Writing Your Own CD-ROMs 141
Kodak Writable CD Applications 144

Chapter 8: The Future of Photo CD 147

Networking 148
Kodak Picture Exchange 150
Kodak's Relationships 152
Kodak's View of Photo CD 154
Welcome to Tomorrow 158

Appendix A: Image Storage and Directories 159

Appendix B: Photo CD Milestones 165

Appendix C: Glossary of Terms 171

Appendix D: List of Manufacturers 191

Index 195

FOREWORD

The marriage of traditional consumer film and computer technologies promises to change the way we live, work, and play—providing new interactive options in entertainment, education, and business.

We at Eastman Kodak Company are proud to be leading a digital imaging revolution with our Photo CD system. For the first time, consumer and commercial customers are now able to store their 35mm and up to 4- by 5-inch film images in digital form on write-once compact discs and view them on television sets or use them in personal computer systems.

Quite simply, the Photo CD system gives the best of two different technologies. It provides the convenience, low cost, and the image quality of traditional photography with the unique advantages of digital technology—the ability to display, enhance, and transmit images electronically.

Jointly developed by Kodak and Philips NV, the Photo CD system had its origin in the late 1980s when Kodak began pursuing the innovative idea of storing images on a write-once compact disc, a product not yet on the market at that time.

Realizing the tremendous potential of a product that could store up to 600 MB of image data and still retain high image quality, Kodak teamed with Philips, an expert in CD technologies, to explore the use of compact discs for image storage. The result of our joint exploration produced the underlying technology for the Photo CD system.

Kodak introduced the Photo CD system in September 1990. Since then, the scope and benefits of Photo CD have been broadened beyond amateur photography, extending the Photo CD concept to mainstream professional, commercial, and medical business users. The additional formats and products demonstrate Kodak's long-range vision for Photo CD technology, as well as the company's commitment to its customers.

We are confident that the Photo CD system will be an integral part of our lives — both in the home and at the office. In the home, consumers can view and edit their Photo CD images on a TV to create custom electronic photo albums. In the commercial market, professionals such as graphic designers, desktop publishers, and multimedia title developers can easily enhance documents, presentations, designs, and titles with Photo CD images.

Business professionals will also be able to create interactive presentations by integrating text, graphics, and sound with images on Photo CD discs.

Today, essentially anyone with a personal computer and a Photo CD-compatible CD-ROM drive has cost-effective and easy access to "digital negatives." By providing new ways to store and use photographs, Kodak is expanding the use of images in our everyday lives, whether at home or at work.

Dr. Leo J. Thomas
President, Imaging
Eastman Kodak Company

INTRODUCTION

At the beginning of this century, George Eastman's introduction of the roll film camera and his slogan, "You push the button, we do the rest," marked the beginning of amateur and general commercial photography.

The roll film and the simple camera began an entire era of photography with inexpensive prints, first in black-and-white and later in color, which became not only part of every home throughout the world, but also led to the development of photography as a major part of advertising, commercial, industrial, medical, and numerous other market applications.

Kodak combined its own technologies and an alliance with Philips NV to develop Photo CD. Now, with the introduction of Photo CD, there is a bridge between conventional silver-halide photography and digital photography based on silicon chips. We are entering a new era where silver and silicon meet—where silver halide images can be easily converted into digital images that are stored on a convenient compact disc. Silver-to-silicon offers the best of each world as they are available today.

Each Photo CD disc can hold up to 100 full-color 35mm photographs. Photo CDs are prepared by photofinishers, professional laboratories, or service bureaus using special equipment to scan images captured on conventional film. The scanned images are then digitally recorded to a writable compact disc. The digital images can be viewed on computer screens or on color television sets. Photo CD is compatible with a variety of television formats, from today's conventional color formats to the proposed high-definition television (HDTV) formats of tomorrow.

The conventional silver-halide color film is an extraordinarily attractive way of capturing an image. To date, no electronic camera can produce an image that can match the resolution and quality of a conventional color film image. Photo CD uses a scanner to create a high-resolution digital image from a film image. This digital image can be enhanced, modified or easily transmitted. These images may be used in a variety of ways—on home television sets, for publishing, or a variety of educational or presentation applications. Perhaps one of the greatest benefits of the Kodak Photo CD system is the convenience it brings to storing and retrieving photographs.

It has been almost three decades since one of the very dramatic changes in film usage occurred—the introduction of the Kodak Instamatic camera, which increased the ease of taking conventional photographs. Today we have autofocusing and auto-exposure 35mm cameras. The number of photo images taken each year has been growing steadily at about 5 percent a year. This year throughout the world more than 50 billion photo images will be taken.

The Photo CD system brings a new dimension to home entertainment. Stored images can be displayed on conventional television sets with players that also can play audio CDs. The Photo CD system not only brings the convenience of home television viewing to conventionally photographed images, but it also brings high-resolution, high-quality color to the world of computing, ranging from desktop publishing to multimedia presentations.

Major photographic companies such as Agfa, Fuji, Konica, and Polaroid have all indicated their support of the Photo CD standard.

Photo CD is an exciting development for both the consumer and the industrial and commercial user of photographic materials. With the support of both the digital and photo industries, the Photo CD image is expected to become a *de facto* standard for future developments in the field of high-quality photographic digital images.

From home entertainment to numerous industrial and scientific applications, Photo CD is a product that offers an excellent transition from film to electronic images.

It is in the spirit of transition that we present this book covering the many elements that make up Photo CD, what can be done with it, what will come in the future, as well as ideas for Photo CD applications.

The opportunities for applying Photo CD are almost endless. People respond eagerly to new ways of using photographs. With the color printers that are available today, it is now possible to include a full-color photograph in a business or personal letter. People are always looking for more ways to use photographs, to view photographs, as well as to reproduce photographs in a variety of ways.

"Kodak developed Photo CD technology to give consumers an exciting, new way to enjoy their pictures, but we didn't stop there," said Stephen S. Stepnes, general manager and vice president of Kodak's CD Imaging business. "We developed the technology with future applications in mind." One example of the design elements of the Photo CD: the Kodak Image Pac file format, which Kodak originally created to store high-resolution 35mm photographic images, was adapted to a wide range of other imaging needs.

"The number of potential commercial uses for Photo CD technology is limited only by the imagination," observed Stepnes. "Although Kodak is already working on a large number of specific applications, we expect that number to multiply rapidly as our customers begin to work with the technology and understand its potential."

For the consumer, Kodak's vice president William Fowble, pointed out, "Photo CD offers a great way to manage your memories. When it comes to organizing and storing prints, most people have good intentions but their pictures never seem to make it out of their closet or dresser drawer."

Photo CD will find exciting applications in wedding photography, commercial photography, industrial photography, and medical photography. Stock photograph houses and the archiving of news photographs are other applications.

Beyond the dimensions of photographs, the writable CD can serve as a medium for sending billing accounts to customers who want the data in digital form. Some companies already receive their telephone bills on compact discs.

While the era of Photo CD is just beginning, the uses for this product will be limited only by the imagination of the users. With its data storage capabilities, new applications will be found for Photo CD—a medium of exceptional quality and form.

John Larish
January 1993

ACKNOWLEDGMENTS

Our deepest gratitude goes to Rose Ellen Larish, who spent many hours at the computer keyboard putting these words together. Our thanks go to the numerous people whose help was beyond measure. A special thanks to Paul McAfee, who arranged the many hours of interviews that were needed and who supplied much of the artwork needed to illustrate this book.

Sincere thanks to others at Kodak, from Stephen Stepnes, who heads Kodak's Photo CD efforts and who is one of the concept's godfathers, to the customer support people who answer the daily stream of questions about Photo CD.

Many people contributed information that helped to make this book complete. Jim Frisch was a great help in understanding the implications of bringing photographs to the printed page. Barbara Roberts of FPG International Corp. helped give a focus to the legal issues that may impact Photo CD. Jukka Ropponen provided Photo CD images and experiential learning relating to new imaging software.

The author wishes to thank the team of editors at Micro Publishing Press who contributed portions of this book, including David Pope, Stephen Beale, and James Cavuoto. Charlene and John Melson contributed some of the photographs in the book; Zzyzx Visual Systems in Los Angeles produced our Photo CDs. Andrew Shalat provided several illustrations and art direction for the cover. Marian Oles took the photo of the author on the cover.

Thanks to all of the people of Kodak and Philips who developed the product, and to those at Agfa, Fuji, Konica, and Polaroid who support it. Thanks for all who share this vision of tomorrow that is here today.

CHAPTER 1

The New Era of Photography

Millions of people throughout the world take pictures of their families, friends, festivities, and vacations with 35mm film cameras. The usual results of their photographic efforts are prints and slides. Some of these prints end up mounted in photo albums, frequently with humorous annotations.

Photographers can examine their slides one at a time in a hand-held viewer, or a slide projector can be set up to display the slides on a screen. Inevitably, many of the prints, negatives, and slides seem to migrate to bottom drawers and shoe boxes and are seldom taken out to be viewed.

More homes have color television sets than slide projectors, so why not view pictures taken with 35mm cameras on a television set? Being able to look at your pictures on a TV is certainly more convenient than having to set up and operate a slide projector in a darkened room. Also, if you can display slides on your television set, then it's just a small step to wanting an easy way to display the same slides on a computer screen.

With Photo CD, Eastman Kodak is providing the bridge from film to electronic screen (Figure 1-1). The Kodak Photo CD system converts images on film into digital form and stores the digital images on a Photo CD disc, which is

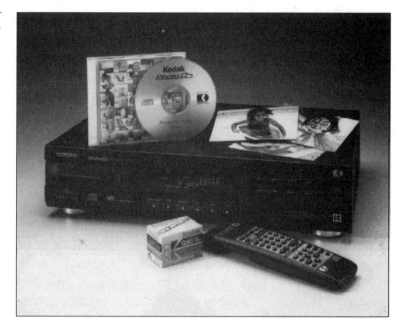

Figure 1-1. Photo CD, jointly developed by Kodak and Philips, allows you to display photographs from a standard 35mm camera on television screens and computer displays. (Courtesy Eastman Kodak Company)

similar to an audio compact disc (CD). Kodak, in partnership with N.V. Philips, has developed a Photo CD player that connects to a television set, and they have also made it possible to use the same Photo CD discs in personal computers that have a compatible CD-ROM drive.

For the amateur photographer, creating pictures for Photo CD is no different than taking slides. No special camera or film is required. At the photofinisher the film is developed as usual and then the images on the film are digitized by a scanner and put onto a Photo CD disc. If desired, slides and prints also can be made (Figure 1-2).

Photo CD is a new means of storing pictures, a new way of managing memories. For the millions of people throughout the world with 35mm cameras, Photo CD offers a modern way of storing and sharing those images with family and friends. Each Photo CD album contains small "thumbnail" prints of the pictures on its cover, so it is easy to see what the disc contains. Each picture is numbered (Figure 1-3).

Figure 1-2. Diagram depicts output options from Kodak Photo CD System. (Courtesy Eastman Kodak Company)

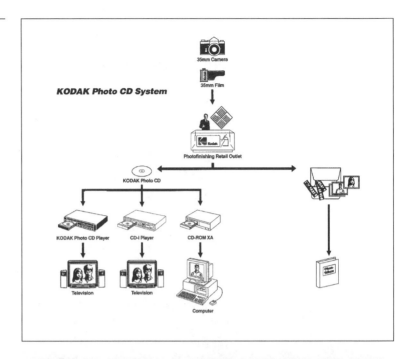

Figure 1-3. The Photo CD case features a numbered thumbnail of each picture on the disc. (Courtesy Eastman Kodak Company)

Using the Photo CD player is similar to using an audio CD player. In fact, the Photo CD player will also play audio CDs, so it can be used to listen to favorite music when you aren't displaying your photographs. Pictures from Photo CD on TV are bright and colorful, and have photographic quality. The brightness and clarity are made possible by the high resolution of the images stored on the Photo CD disc. The resolution is so high that Photo CD images can be shown on the new, high-definition television (HDTV) sets without the need for any modification to the stored images.

Just as songs on an audio CD can be played in any order, pictures on a Photo CD do not have to be displayed in the sequence in which they are stored or numbered. The Photo CD player can not only be programmed to play images in any desired sequence, but it also remembers the sequences for future playing. This latter feature is like having an electronic slide carousel. Pictures on the screen can be resized to show details, and these changescan be saved in the player for later viewing.

To view Photo CD images on a computer, the user needs a Photo CD-compatible CD-ROM XA drive. The computer can not only be used to view the Photo CD pictures, but it also can be used to enhance or alter the images and then store them in other computer files. Kodak has developed computer software for using Photo CD images in desktop publishing applications (see Chapter Five).

For the professional photographer, Photo CD offers not only storage and photo enhancement capabilities, but also new marketing possiblities such as Photo CD albums for weddings, graduations, and anniversaries.

It is in the commercial field where Photo CD is expected to find its greatest use. Commercial applications will appear in almost every field of business activity, from artists' portfolios and real estate listings to medical records and multimedia catalogs.

Photo CD is natural partner for electronic publishing because it gives publishers a low-cost and practical means for obtaining and storing photograph-quality color images in digital form. Photo CD is expected to play a major role in the production of newspapers, magazines, and books. In offices, Photo CD color images will be added to reports, documents, and even sales letters. Engineering documents will incorporate Photo CD color images, and the engineering documents themselves can be stored on writable CD discs. In the classroom, teachers will be able to quickly select and display individual pictures from a Photo CD disc, or they can use Photo CD to create presentations that show the pictures in the desired sequence.

The potential for Photo CD goes far beyond amateur and professional photography. While developing Photo CD, Kodak decided to create an entire imaging system rather than just the photography application. By extending Photo CD to computers, Kodak has opened the way for widespread use of the technology. Business, education, medicine, engineering, and publishing—in all of these areas, Photo CD has the potential for becoming a part of the normal day-to-day operations.

What Is Photo CD?

Photo CD is a system. The core of the Photo CD system is the Photo CD disc and the technology used to store digital images on the disc. To this core, Kodak has added a wide range of products designed to meet the different needs of the home user and the various commercial markets.

The basic Photo CD disc holds up to 100 images that have been digitized from 35mm film. The images are stored at five resolution levels, ranging from low-resolution thumbnail pictures to high-resolution images that can be used for color printing. Each Photo CD disc is packaged in a "jewel case." The cover of the case has indexed thumbnail prints that serve as a guide for accessing the images that are stored on the disc. Each thumbnail image is numbered to correspond to an image recorded on the disc. The same Photo CD disc can be used in a Photo CD player, CD-Interactive (CD-I) player, or a computer CD-ROM XA drive.

For the home user, there is the Kodak Photo CD player, which comes in several models with different control features. Photo CD players from other manufacturers such as Philips can be expected to offer their own special features.

Home users will find a variety of Photo CD players in retail stores. Home Photo CD users who have personal computers will be able to buy CD-ROM drives that will enable them to view and manipulate the digitized Photo CD images on their computer screens.

For the professional and commercial markets, the Kodak Photo CD system has been expanded to provide specialized formats for professional photographers, multimedia presentations, catalogs, and medical images. In addition, Kodak has extended the Photo CD system to include imaging hardware and software.

Hardware products include CD-ROM drives, a system that allows a computer to record images on an optical compact disc, digital cameras, film scanners, and continuous-tone color printers. Kodak is marketing software products for Photo CD image access and manipulation, image enhancment, color management, page layout, and management of image libraries (Figure 1-4).

The Photo CD system begins with the color film in a camera and ends with the viewing of images. The system has many branches, with each branch requiring its own equipment and supporting tools, but the common factor is the digital image stored on a Photo CD disc. The final product of Photo

Figure 1-4. Kodak markets several software products that work with Photo CD.

CD is viewing those images, and Photo CD allows the images to be viewed in a variety of ways: on a TV or computer screen, projected onto a large screen, or printed on paper.

Capabilities of Photo CD

The capabilities required by the various branches of the Photo CD system are different. The needs of the home Photo CD user are not the same as those of the professional photographer or a graphic designer. Kodak has addressed this problem by developing specialized equipment and tools for several different business applications of Photo CD.

Home Use

In the home, the Photo CD player used to display photographs on a television set is also capable of zooming in, enlarging, cropping, and manipulating images on the screen. These choices can be kept in the player's memory, and when the Photo CD disc is played again, the edited versions of the photographs will be automatically displayed. The sequence of images to be displayed also can be kept in memory, in effect, creating an instant photo album.

If a Photo CD disc is not full, it can be brought back to the photofinisher to have more pictures added to it until the limit is reached. Discs that are recorded more than once are called multi-session discs. A multi-session disc may not hold the full complement of 100 picture because part of the space is needed to record the control data needed by the Photo CD player or computer.

Presentations

In addition to digital photographs, a Photo CD format called Portfolio also supports text, sound, and graphics, all of which are merged into television-resolution images that can be used for multimedia presentations. Photographs from a Photo CD disc can be duplicated to a Portfolio disc along with text titles, accompanying sound, and graphics. Portfolio discs can be played on Photo CD players and computer CD-ROM drives.

Kodak has developed an authoring system that allows Photo CD users to create complete programs of pictures, sound, and text on their computers and send this information on floppy discs to a Photo CD service bureau for the production of Portfolio discs.

Professional Use

For the professional photographer, Kodak has developed a special disc format called the Pro Photo CD Master, which can store images from larger format films (up to 4 by 5 inches) as well as 35mm film. Photographers can also use the Photo CD Portfolio disc format to create multimedia products by adding sound, graphics, and text to their photographs.

Graphic designers and publishers, as well as photographers, will find that the combination of Photo CD and a computer can be used as an "electronic darkroom." Images stored on Photo CD discs can be brought up on the computer screen, then cropped, resized, and placed into a computer file. With imaging software, the photographer can alter the images by removing unwanted objects, changing selected colors, and making other types of enhancements. Using the "electronic darkroom," a photographer can make changes in photographs that are difficult or impossible to do in an actual darkroom.

Kodak has developed software packages to enable professional photographers and other Photo CD users to access, manage, and enhance images from a Photo CD library. Many of the widely used illustration and publishing software packages can also be used to manipulate and alter Photo CD images.

Two other Photo CD disc formats are available from Kodak. The catalog format allows up to 6000 images to be stored on a single disc along with text, graphics, and sound. The data can be organized and accessed as pages. Integrated into each catalog disc is special software that allows the user to browse through the information.

Kodak has announced a medical disc format designed for storing X-ray film images and other diagnostic images at full resolution. The possibility of storing the medical records of patients with their diagnostic images is being explored.

Photo CD Hardware

Kodak is also marketing the imaging equipment that is needed to operate and use the Photo CD system. For photofinishers, Kodak provides a special film scanner for digitizing 35mm pictures, a laser-powered writer for recording the images on Photo CD discs, a printer for producing the thumbnail index prints, and a computer workstation for controlling the entire process. A large-format film scanner for handling film sizes up to 4 by 5 inches is also available from Kodak.

Photo CD users who want to digitize images on 35mm film themselves can purchase desktop film scanners from Kodak or other scanner makers. If they want to eliminate the need

Figure 1-5. Kodak's Professional Digital Camera System 200.

for both film and scanning, they buy a digital camera from Kodak, Sony, or other manufacturers. Kodak's professional digital camera can be connected directly to a computer (Figure 1-5).

Kodak has introduced a PCD Writer that can record images and data from a computer on a write-once compact disc. The PCD Writer also can be used to read data from Photo CD and CD-ROM discs.

For those who want to output the digital images on Photo CD discs or in the computer as prints or transparencies, Kodak and other companies offer dye-transfer color printers that produce high-quality, continuous-tone pictures. The more expensive laser copier-printers, such as the Kodak ColorEdge and Canon CLC 500, also can produce high-quality prints from computer-based Photo CD images.

Image management and retrieval—being able to quickly find and retrieve specific images—is another capability that Kodak is providing for the Photo CD system. Kodak's Professional Image Library system can handle up to 100 Photo CD discs and 10,000 images. The user enters key words to search the library. Pictures that fit the search criteria are brought up on screen as low-resolution thumbnail images, any of which can be selected for viewing, editing, or printing at full resolution.

Potential for Photo CD

We all know the folk saying, "A picture is worth a thousand words." Tomorrow, when family pictures are stored on Photo CD discs, some of us may end up saying, "This picture is worth 18 megabytes."

Consumer Photography
Worldwide, more than 60 billion pictures per year are taken with 35mm cameras. Because these cameras are so

familiar and easy to use, and 35mm film produces high-quality pictures at low-cost, people will continue to use film cameras to record the events in their lives (Figure 1-6). It also seems likely that these people will find it natural to view their family photographs on another familiar imaging device—the color television set.

Photo CD has the potential for bringing photography and television together in millions of homes. With the Photo CD player, a viewer can select any sequence of images from the 100 stored on the disc. Once a sequence has been selected, it can be stored for future replays—in effect, creating an electronic photo album. Simply by choosing a different sequence, another "album" can be created from images on the same disc.

Home users can ask the photofinisher to add their own voice, music, drawings, and titles to any of the images on a disc. Family albums on Photo CD Portfolio discs could become multimedia presentations. Other multimedia family album possibilities are weddings, births, childhood events, graduations, and family reunions.

Figure 1-6. Photo CD will co-exist with conventional photography for some time to come.

This capability to choose or program images and the capability to enlarge and crop images gives the user interactive control of the medium, and could provide the home users of Photo CD with a viewing pleasure that is not possible with slides or photographic prints.

Business Computing

In business, commercial, and industrial offices, computers have completely changed the way in which information is handled, generated, and communicated. Word processing and database software have become an essential part of office procedures, and the next generation of computer technology is bringing imaging and multimedia capabilities to the office. Photo CD is part of this advance into imaging and multimedia.

The CD-ROM drive has removed a major barrier for the use of color images on computers. Color pictures, when stored on magnetic media, take up a tremendous amount of the available memory. When digitized, a single color slide can take up 18 megabytes, and a full-page, four-color image can take up 30 megabytes or more.

Another barrier to the widespread use of color images in computers is the relatively high cost of scanners used for digitizing color pictures. A color scanner can cost as much as high-powered color computer system.

What Photo CD offers is easy access to high-quality digital images that can be used on computers. Photo CD and other CD-ROM discs are conveniently small but big in memory capacity—up to 650 megabytes. Photo CD discs can be played on Photo CD-compatible CD-ROM drives, which are increasingly being used for operating large databases. Also, with Photo CD, instead of having to buy an expensive color scanner and learn how to use it, companies can take advantage of the low-cost digitizing service provided by Photo CD service bureaus.

Photo CD fits into the trend to color imaging in business computing. Many offices already have installed the hardware and software needed for handling color images along with text and graphics. Kodak has been working closely with many of the leading computer hardware and software manufacturers to establish standards and to make Photo CD compatible with the most widely used office computer products. Acceptance of Photo CD as a standard for storing digitized images could have a major impact on the emerging market for computer imaging products.

Kodak has negotiated agreements for Photo CD with major computer product vendors, including Apple Computer, Lotus, Novell, and Electronics for Imaging. Philips, Pioneer, Sony, and Toshiba have announced that the CD-ROM drives they manufacture will be compatible with the Photo CD format.

Kodak has laid the groundwork for introducing Photo CD into the office and has developed versions of Photo CD to meet the needs of special segments of the business and professional markets. In addition, Kodak is developing tools to help business users of Photo CD. The potential for Photo CD in the business marketplace is almost unlimited. A major driving force will be commercial applications that can be developed with Photo CD. As in any emerging market, the greatest opportunities lie in the early phase—and it has just begun!

Printing and Publishing

In the past decade, there has been an explosion in the number of four-color pages that are printed annually. The cost of color printing has dropped and part of the drop in cost is due to the introduction of what has been termed desktop publishing. Desktop publishing took page production away from the printer and the printing trade shops and brought it into the office. At first, desktop publishing software was used to compose type, then page layout and illustration placement was added, followed by image editing and color separation capabilities.

A limiting factor in using the computer for preparing color pages has been the lack of a suitable medium for storing digitized color images. Photo CD has been designed to fill that need.

Publishers have a new tool in Photo CD that can give them high-quality images at low cost. Editors of publications such as newsletters, yearbooks, small magazines, and community newspapers can use a local photofinisher as a low-cost service bureau for scanning and digitizing color photographs. Glossy magazines that need very high resolution digital images can get them from the Pro Photo CD discs that have been designed for use by professional photographers.

Photo CD offers an alternative to printing. Products such as catalogs can be produced as interactive Photo CD discs. So could illustrated books and picture magazines. However, it is likely that the most successful electronic publishing products have yet to be invented. We are still learning how to use the powerful multimedia capabilities of Photo CD.

Medicine and Medical Education

Kodak's Photo CD technology is being extended to provide a means for storing medical images. The Kodak Photo CD Medical format will allow both film-based images, such as medical photographs and X-rays, and digital images, such as computed tomography (CT) and magnetic resonance (MR) to be stored on CDs, along with related patient records.

The new medical CD format will maintain compatibility with the American College of Radiology and National Electrical Manufacturers Association (ACR-NEMA) format for diagnostic imaging. Image and patient information will be assembled into ACR-NEMA files on Kodak Photo CD Medical discs.

The Photo CD medical technology also is being integrated into the Kodak Ektascan Imagelink system, which was developed with Vortech Data, Inc. The Ektascan Imagelink system is capable of capturing, networking, storing, and retrieving diagnostic images and patient data.

Working with the Mallinckrodt Institute of Radiology at Washington University Medical Center in St. Louis and other leading medical institutions the Kodak Health Sciences Division is developing ways to use the Photo CD medical disc technology in medical education and training. Other potential medical applications of Photo CD are in pathology, dermatology, and storing medical lab results.

Advertising Agencies

Kodak's Picture Exchange network (see Chapter Eight) has sparked interest in the advertising community. The possibility of on-line access to photographs and other images from around the world opens new vistas for ad creation.

Burt Manning, chairman and chief executive officer of J. Walter Thompson, said, "Our art buyers and directors constantly search for the perfect image to present creative concepts to our clients. Kodak Picture Exchange will simplify and improve our photo searches, saving us time and money. The potential advantages are so great we intend to test the Kodak Picture Exchange thoroughly and anticipate that our key image providers will soon be a part of the system."

Joseph DeDeo, Young & Rubicam's group vice president, vice chairman, and chief creative officer, said, "We are delighted to see that Eastman Kodak Company is providing the industry leadership necessary to set new standards for the scanning, indexing, storage, and exchange of high-quality pictures. We look forward to having an early opportunity to use the Kodak Picture Exchange service and plan to evaluate other Photo CD products."

Markets for Photo CD

Photo CD offers many advantages for casual and professional photographers, but they are not the only ones to benefit. By bringing high-quality digital photographs to television screens and computing systems, the Photo CD System is making it possible for home and business users to take advantage of images in ways never before possible. With Kodak Photo CD technologies, the imaging and information industries can develop a wide variety of new products.

The Photo CD System marks a real revolution in business communication. A black-and-white, text-based world will be transformed into one where color photographs are commonplace. Presentations, letters, memos and reports will all be enhanced by the addition of high-quality Photo CD images.

The general markets for Photo CD include:

- Home use for the storage and playback of 35mm film generated images.

- Industrial and commercial use for the storage and retrieval of high-quality images for publishing and presentations.

- Catalog publishing, both retail and wholesale.

- Electronic publishing.

- Medical storage of photo images and diagnostic digital images.

- Education and libraries for storage and display of photographs, graphs, charts along with sound.

Application Ideas for Photo CD

Here are some application ideas for Photo CD you will find in later chapters of this book:

Advertising Agency Showcase—Advertising agencies can create customized showcases of their work on Photo CD discs to show to prospective clients (see page 51).

Artist Portfolio—Artists and art galleries can create portfolios on Photo CD discs to show their works of art to buyers (see page 145).

Books on Photo CD—Book publishers have already begun to include images from their books on a Photo CD. Publishers can also sounds to the disc (see page C-5)

Business-to-Business Product Directories—Commercial and industrial supply catalogs can run to over a thousand pages. Putting them on Catalog Photo CD discs with photos and text will make the information more accessible. (see page 96).

Catalogs on Disk—Home shoppers will be able to browse through electronic catalogs using Photo CD's Catalog discs (see page 112).

Civic Event Portfolios—Local civic celebrations, parades, festivals, fairs, meetings, conventions, sports days, and homecomings can be captured on Portfolio discs with photos, sound, and text. (see page C-8).

Classroom Displays—Teachers can use the branching capabilities of Photo CD to display suitable pictures as they teach. The teacher can display on television or use a projection device. (see page C-5).

Clip-Art Photographs—Up to 100 full color photographs on a disc and reproduction rights are being sold by some vendors. Others allow reproduction of lower resolution images but encrypt the high-resolution version so they can charge a royalty. (see page 121).

Corporate Image Libraries—Companies with large libraries of photographs can store them on Photo CD discs and then access them quickly using a computer to search for specific images. (see page 90).

Family Milestones—Snapshots of family events such as birthdays, anniversaries, graduation, and vacations can be combined with voice, music and graphics to create lasting memories. (see page 22).

Family Portraits on Disc—Portrait photos of children can be added to a Photo CD disc as they grow up. Family portraits can be kept together on a disc to create a continuing family record. (see page C-1).

Genealogy Record—Family trees illustrated with photographs can be stored on Photo CD discs, with branching to show different lines of descent. On Portfolio discs, sound and graphics can be added. The family tree CDs can be replicated for family members. (see page C-3).

Insurance Documentation—Photographs of insured property along with relevant supporting documentation can be stored on Photo CD discs. Insurance claim adjusters can use Photo CD to record photographs of damage. (see page C-7).

Interior Design Showcase—Interior designers and furniture vendors can use Photo CD to show a wide variety of products in color. (see page 158).

Lecture Presentations—Photo CD discs can be used instead of slides to illustrate a lecture or talk. A sequence can be programmed or the speaker can choose to display any of the images on the disc. (see page 157).

Medical Records—Permanent patient medical records, including X-rays and diagnostic images, can be stored on Photo CD discs. (see page 143).

Museum Kiosks—Conversion of collections to Photo CDs is beginning because of image quality. Photo CDs are finding their way into helpful museum Kiosks for visitor use. (see page 70).

Newspaper Morgue—Journalists used the macabre term morgue to refer to the reference library the contained all of the published (i.e. dead) stories and other reference material. The modern newspaper morgue is likely to be found on a CD-ROM. (see page 103).

Photo Albums—Photo CD offers a more convenient storage medium than a shoebox or desk drawer for creating photo albums (see page C-4).

Professional Photographers Sales Tool—Using the Photo CD Catalog or Portfolio discs, professional photographers can send their work to clients—or prospective clients—for review. (see page 138).

Real Estate Listings— Photographs of the exterior and interior of property for sale can be shown in any sequence to clients in their homes or in the agent's office. Photo CD images can be used for printed listings and the images can be transmitted to other offices and even out of state. (see page C-2).

Retailer Kiosks—Self-service kiosks with color photographs, text, and voice will enable retail stores to offer shoppers a new way to browse or search through a wide range of products. (see page 127).

Stock Photos Catalogs— Stock photo houses can send clients Photo CD discs with low-resolution images and supply the high-resolution version after an agreement has been reached. (see page 123).

Trade Show Kiosks—Manufacturers can augment their trade show displays with a Photo-CD based kiosk that shows their entire line in full color. (see page 72).

Training Manuals—Companies are converting their printed training manuals into "talking slide presentations" that can be stored on Photo CDs. (see page 149).

Yearbooks on Disc—High school yearbooks can now be more easily produced using digital Photo CD images. New products can be created supplementing yearbooks with sound and picture Portfolio discs. (see page C-6).

Bridge to the Future

Photo CD is a simple but elegant bridge to the world of digital photography. It creates a new world where silver and silicon meet, making use of the best features of film and digital imaging to create a new way to store high-quality color photographs. Widespread use of Photo CD can make it a *de facto* standard for digital images.

At the end of this decade, a new century begins. Kodak with the introduction of Photo CD is settting a course to a future in which digital imaging will play an increasing part in our daily work and lives. Photo CD is here and available today, and offers everybody a convenient and inexpensive way to begin working with digital images.

CHAPTER 2

How Photo CD Works

Kodak announced the Photo CD system in 1990, and today the product is ready for use in the home, office, industry, and studio (Figure 2-1). The marriage of traditional film and computer technologies in Photo CD promises to change the way we live, work, and play. Photo CD provides us with a new interactive "multimedium" that has hundreds of practical applications in entertainment, education, and business.

Photo CD System technology was developed jointly by the Eastman Kodak Company and N.V. Philips. Kodak's efforts were directed to the quality of the image, while

Figure 2-1. The original Kodak Photo CD Master disc on the left. Kodak Pro Photo CD Master discs store images from 35mm and larger formats. Kodak Photo CD Portfolio discs allow the creation of on-disc programs with pictures, text, graphics, and sound. Kodak Photo CD Catalog discs allow easy distribution of disc catalogs containing up to 6000 images. Kodak Photo CD Medical discs can store diagnostic images.

Philips' experience with CD-ROM was a key part of the development process. Philips developed and published the standard for Photo CD as part of the *Orange Book*, one of a series of CD standards books published by Philips for licensees of CD technology.

Family Memories on Disc

APPLICATION BRIEF

Snapshots of family events such as birthdays, anniversaries, vacations, holiday visits, and family reunions can be combined with voices, music, and graphics on Photo CD Portfolio discs to create lasting memories for all family members.

Snapshots of favorite pets and children's antics taken over the years can be assembled on single Photo CD discs, making easy to review fond moments and events.

A typical family snapshot. (Courtesy Jukka Ropponen)

Photo CD Disc Formats

Five Photo CD disc formats (Figure 2-2) have been introduced by Kodak:

Photo CD Master

This original format for home and office applications can store up to 100 digitized color images. The film is digitized in a scanner, and the scanned image is stored on the disc in five different resolution levels. "Base" resolution is equivalent to the resolution of current TV sets. There are two resolutions lower than base, and two that are higher. Base and lower resolutions are stored without data compression. The two higher resolutions are stored in a compressed form to save disc space. The lowest, Base/16, is for thumbnail proofs, and the highest, 16X, gives full photographic resolution. Options include addition of text, graphics, and sound.

Figure 2-2. Kodak Photo CD formats.

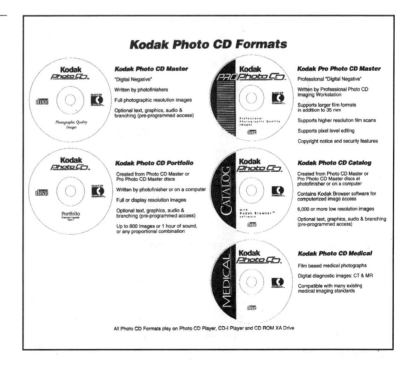

Pro Photo CD Master

Developed for professional photographers, this format can store digitized images scanned from 4 by 5-inch film as well as from 120 and 35mm film. A new large-format scanner is used. The full-resolution images on the Pro disc are not compatible with the regular Photo CD Master format, but the lower resolution images are compatible. The Pro format allows copyright notices to be embedded in the images and also offers encryption and watermarking.

Photo CD Portfolio

This format is intended for viewing images at TV or computer screen resolution. Up to 800 TV-resolution images can be stored on the disc, or over one hour of sound. Text and graphics, as well as audio, can be added to the images, but this decreases the number of images that can be stored on the disc. This format is suited for multimedia presentations. Users can create the sequences using Kodak's authoring software on their computers or the authoring can be done on the photofinisher's Photo CD workstation.

Photo CD Catalog

This format can store up to 6000 images formatted into catalog pages with text, graphics, and sound. Browsing software included on every disc allows keyword searches on Macintosh or PC computers.

Photo CD Medical

Customized for medical applications, this format can store diagnostic film images, such as X-rays, at full resolution. This eliminates the need to keep the original films on hand. The format allows digital diagnostic images, such as CT and MR scans, to be stored on the disc as well. The format conforms to medical image data standards.

All of the new formats can be used on Photo CD players as well as compatible CD-ROM drives on computers. This is the common thread that makes Photo CD potentially a *de facto* standard for storing digital images. The Photo CD

System makes available an affordable access to high-quality digital images.

Today, analog and digital still cameras do not have the resolution of the 35mm film camera. Many experts predict that it will be well into the 21st century before digital cameras approach film resolution and also have the capacity needed to store color image data equal to that in a single frame of 35mm film. A single 35mm color slide is estimated to contain about 250 megabytes of data.

Photo CD Master Image Format

Surprisingly, the 35mm film frame is not 35 millimeters in size. Each 35mm film frame is 36 mm by 24 mm, and the Photo CD Master image retains that 3:2 ratio (Figure 2-3).

Each image on a Photo CD Master disc is created from an array of square pixels, or picture elements. Colors are encoded using a color model that defines color space in terms of x, y, and z coordinates.

Figure 2-3. The scan area covered in a Photo CD.

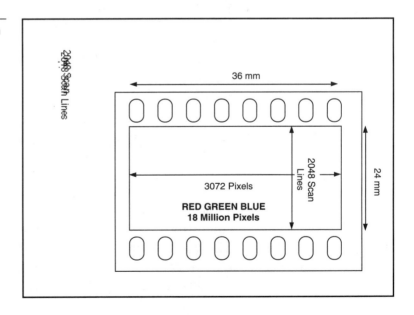

36 mm

24 mm

2048 Scan Lines

3072 Pixels

RED GREEN BLUE
18 Million Pixels

Every image is stored at five resolutions. Base resolution is the equivalent of the resolution of current television screens. Other resolutions are derived from Base in multiples of 4 or 16. Base/4 is one-fourth of Base resolution, and Base/16 is one-sixteenth of Base. Base and the two lower resolutions are stored without data compression; 4 Base (four times Base) and 16 Base (16 times Base) resolutions are not stored as full images. Instead they are stored as compressed residuals—in other words, as the differences between the uncompressed Base and the higher resolution.

Base/16, or Level 1, has a resolution of 128 lines by 192 pixels and is used for thumbnails and contact sheets. Base/4, or Level 2, has a resolution of 256 lines by 384 pixels. Level 3, or Base, is used for creating an image at TV resolution. Level 4, or 4 Base, provides an image for high-definition TV. Level 5, or 16 Base, provides photographic-quality images with a resolution of 2048 lines by 3072 pixels.

Colors are encoded using PhotoYCC, a color model developed by Kodak for Photo CD. PhotoYCC defines colors in terms of luminance (the black and white, or brightness, component) and chrominance (the color component). The Y is roughly equivalent to luminance, and the CC represents color differences, one red minus Y and the other blue minus Y. This kind of color coding is used in broadcasting television signals. It allows a monochrome TV to display a black and white image and ignore the color signals. Because we cannot see a point as red and green at the same time, the red TV signal can be used to define green. The same is possible for the opposite colors blue and yellow.

The color-encoding scheme used in PhotoYCC is defined in terms of a reference device. This reference device can sense and quantify almost every color in a scene that is recorded by traditional photography. The encoding separates each color pixel into one 8-bit luma (brightness) component and two 8-bit chroma (color channel) components.

A color defined by PhotoYCC can be readily converted to RGB (red, green, blue) signals for video display and conversely RGB signals from a color scanner can be converted into PhotoYCC values. Kodak has extended the color space used for television to allow Photo CD to specify colors that cannot be created with the RGB phosphors on a screen but can be created by printing the images. PhotoYCC provides a sufficient range of signal levels and the color gamut (range of color values) needed to support high-quality printing devices.

The hierarchy of components that compose a single image is stored on the disc in what is called an Image Pac. Image Pacs comprise the majority of data recorded on the Photo CD Master disc. The average size of a Photo CD Image Pac for a 35mm image is 4.5 megabytes (MB), a very efficient amount of space for a high-quality photograph. However, depending upon the film type used and the scene content, the actual size of an Image Pac can range from 3 to 6 MB. Typically, 100 images will fit on a standard-size 120mm disc (Figure 2-4).

Figure 2-4. The contribution of the various elements to an average image size.

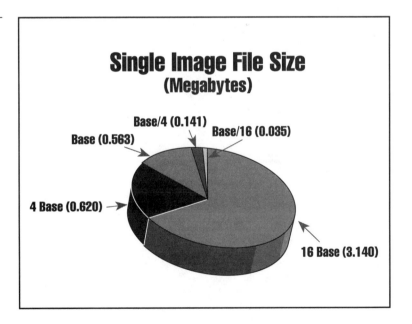

Figure 2-5.
Photofinishers will use the Kodak Photo CD Imaging Workstation 2400 with a second disc writer that triples production.

Figure 2-6. A flow diagram of the Kodak Photo CD Imaging Workstation 2400.

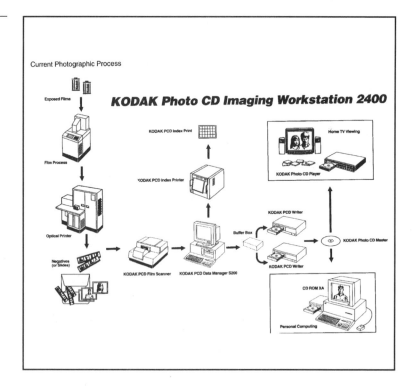

Additional information recorded on the disc, including Microcontroller Readable Sectors (MRS) in each Image Pac, makes it possible to use the discs without a computer. The additional sectors provide operating information to Photo CD players, and this allows the player units to be built without a computer inside.

Kodak also made Photo CD discs compatible with standard CD-ROM drives used in computers. To accommodate Photo CD discs for general use in computer systems, each Image Pac on the disc is represented in accordance to the ISO 9660:1988 international standard.

How Photos CDs Are Mastered

Photofinishers use a Kodak Photo CD imaging workstation to digitize 35mm film images (slides, color negatives, or black-and-white negatives) or small prints up to 4 by 6 inches. The digitized image data is passed from the scanner to a computer workstation, which controls the scanner, Photo CD disc writer, and color printer used to produce thumbnails for the disc case. This color printer also can produce photograph-quality prints from the full-resolution images on the Photo CD disc (Figures 2-5 and 2-6).

The workstation makes conversions from RGB scanner output to the PhotoYCC color space, and then encodes the image data for the five different resolutions files that are stored on the disc.

The disc authoring station has five basic components: a film scanner, workstation, disc writer, color printer, and disc reader. The Kodak PCD Scanner digitizes film negatives or slides in less than 5 seconds per image. The scanning resolution is 2048 lines by 3072 pixels at 12 bits (4096 shades) per primary color (Figure 2-7).

Figure 2-7. The Kodak PCD Scanner.

Figure 2-8. The Kodak PCD Data Manager.

Figure 2-9. The Kodak PCD Writer.

Figure 2-10. The Kodak PCD Index Printer.

The Photo CD computer workstation, called the PCD Data Manager 100, is a Sun SPARC workstation with Kodak software (Figure 2-8). It encodes image data and automatically performs the color and density adjustments on the image data.

The Kodak PCD Writer (Figure 2-9) is used to record the image data on the Photo CD Master disc. The writer has a laser that burns tiny holes on the disc that represent the digital data of the image. Photo CD data, once recorded on the disc, cannot be altered in the same way that data on a magnetic disk can be changed. Once the holes are burned into the disc, they remain there. If the image is altered, a new pattern of holes has to be recorded elsewhere on the disc.

Thumbnail index prints for the Photo CD Master case, as well as photographic-quality standard-size prints and enlargements up to 100 inches square can be produced by the Photo CD color printer (Figure 2-10). The disc reader is a CD-ROM XA drive for the computer workstation. It is used to check newly recorded Photo CD discs, and to read Photo CD discs to make copies, prints, and enlargements.

If an entire Photo CD Master is recorded in one session, as many as 118 scanned images can be included on a single disc. Each additional recording of images onto the disc will reduce storage capacity by four images (Figure 2-11). About 18 megabytes are required on the disc for control information for each session that is recorded.

Television Display

To display Photo CD Master images on television sets, consumers have their choice of several models of Photo CD players from Kodak (Figure 2-12). Other consumer CD systems, such as Philips CD-I systems, will also be able to

Figure 2-11. The capacity of the Photo CD is related to the number of sessions recorded on a single disc. If a single session is recorded filling the disc, 118 images can be recorded. The more sessions, the lower the capacity.

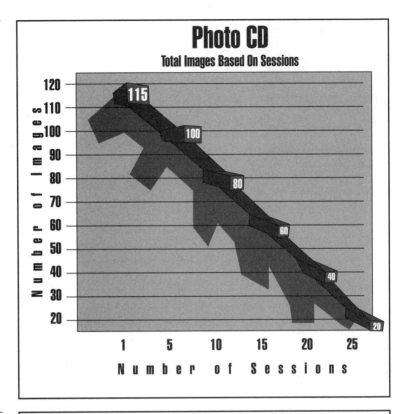

Figure 2-12. The Photo CD player uses a laser beam to read the information stored on the disc and light reflected from removed "pits" are read by a photo detector.

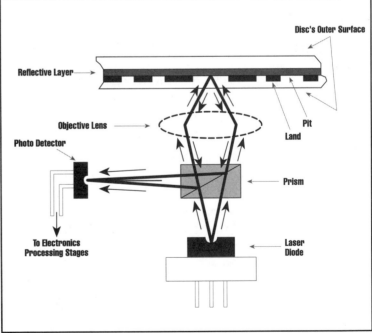

Figure 2-13. The Philips Compact Disc-Interactive System can play Photo CDs.

play Photo CD Master discs (Figure 2-13). Both the Kodak and the CD-Interactive players are able to play standard audio CDs.

Once the Photo CD player has been connected to a television set, the user simply drops in a disc and begins viewing. Specific images can be selected with the remote control device or by using the buttons on the player. The viewer can zoom in and out, or pan through the displayed image. Future Photo CD players may also have features such as high-speed search and programmed play of Photo CD images.

Photo CD Master discs—like audio CDs—can be recorded and played anywhere in the world. Photo CD players are compatible with current international television formats and the new high-definition television formats.

Kodak offers several models of Photo CD players. The Kodak Photo CD Player Model PCD 270 has an "autoplay" feature that automatically displays selected images at intervals of two seconds. Another feature, "keep," remembers the way photos were last viewed on TV, eliminating the need to program a disc each time it is played. The "skip" function deletes a photograph from the playback sequence (but it remains on the disc for future viewing). "Favorite picture selection," or FPS, remembers all of the edits and viewing selections, so that the disc plays the same way on subsequent viewings.

The Kodak Photo CD Player Model PCD 870 is a deluxe unit with expanded features. One example is the "2X tele" feature that allows users to select a rectangular portion of an image and enlarge it. The "FPS" feature of the PCD 870 player has an expanded memory (from 2K to 8K) for remembering edits on discs. In addition, the "full view" feature compensates for the different aspect ratio of a TV screen and a 35mm photograph, displaying the complete

Figure 2-14. The Kodak PCD 5870 player features a five-disc carousel.

35mm image on screen with no "bleed" or image loss at the edge.

The Kodak Photo CD Player Model PCD 5870 (Figure 2-14) offers all the features of the PCD 870 player plus a five-disc carousel. It also features on-screen display of the image number, which allows for easy indexing and fast photo identification.

Professional Use of Photo CD

Professional photographers using large-format films can store their images in digital form on Pro Photo CD discs. This format makes available to these photographers all the features of the standard Kodak Photo CD Master disc and also provides additional features to meet their professional requirements.

Like the standard Kodak Photo CD Master format, the Kodak Pro Photo CD Master format allows 35mm negatives or slides to be scanned onto compact discs at full photographic resolution. The images can then be viewed on a TV set using a Photo CD or CD-I player. But more likely, the photographer or client will want to work with the image on a computer, which can be done by putting the disc into the computer's CD-ROM drive.

The Kodak Pro Photo CD Master format can store 35mm, 120, and 4x5-inch images at resolutions up to 4000 by 6000 pixels. The higher resolution capability of the Pro scanner and Pro discs allows the digitized images to retain the fine detail desired by professional photographers. The Pro format will support 8 x 10-inch film image files, and Kodak is considering future products to take advantage of this capability.

The images on the Pro disc can be edited on a Kodak Professional Photo CD workstation and returned to the Pro disc. The professional format is the only Photo CD disc format that allows digitally enhanced images to be returned to a Kodak Photo CD Master disc. Each Pro disc can store from 25 to 100 images, depending on the scanning resolution and film size.

Making Pro Photo CDs

Images are scanned onto Kodak Pro Photo CD Master discs using the Kodak Professional Photo CD film scanner 4045, which handles professional film up to 4 x 5-inches. The scanner is part of the Kodak Professional PCD Imaging Workstation 4200 (Figure 2-15).

The new 4045 film scanner is capable of digitizing color negatives, color transparencies, and black-and-white negatives with the fine detail required by professional photographers. The scanner has a linear CCD (charge-coupled device) array of 4000 elements, allowing scans at up to 4000 pixels by 6000 lines. The tri-color linear array with 12-bit sampling produces images with 24 bits, or 16.7 million colors. The scan of a single 4 x 5-inch image can produce a

Figure 2-15. The Kodak Professional Photo CD Imaging Workstation 4200 enables professional labs to create Kodak Pro Photo CD Master discs.

72-MB file. The unit is fast, completing 4000 by 6000 pixel scans in 90 seconds and 2000 by 3000 pixel scans in 45 seconds.

Like the Photo CD workstation used by consumer photofinishers, the Kodak professional imaging workstation is a complete system that can be operated by one person. It consists of five components: a film scanner, workstation computer, compact disc writer, CD-ROM XA drive, and thermal printer (Figure 2-16). The professional workstation and the 4045 film scanner can also be used to produce Photo CD Master discs.

After a film image has been scanned, the workstation transforms the raw data into Photo CD files and records the images on a Pro Master disc using the compact disc writer. The Pro Master discs can store photographs taken on a variety of film sizes, including 35mm, 70mm, 120, and 4 x 5-inch. Up to 4000 by 6000 pixel images can be stored on a single Pro disc.

The Pro Photo CD scanning process can be adjusted to accommodate the wide variety of professional films by

Figure 2-16. Flow diagram of the Kodak Professional Photo CD Imaging Workstation 4200.

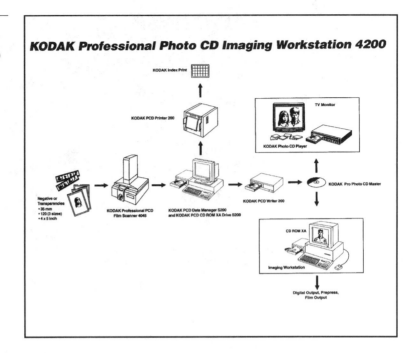

using sophisticated look-up tables. This feature allows the digitized image to retain the effect or "look" the photographer created on film.

The professional workstation can also be networked to other computers that are being used for image editing. For example, someone using a Macintosh or PC to modify a Photo CD image can send the edited image via the network to the Kodak professional workstation, which can then record the edited image on a Pro Photo CD disc.

Security Features

The Pro Photo CD system offers important security features to professional photographers. Software for the professional workstation enables the photographer to put copyright notices on images and to protect images on the Pro disc from unauthorized use.

Each image on a Kodak Pro Photo CD Master disc can be marked with a special identifier that can contain the photographer's name and copyright, as well as other information. For security, images can be watermarked (with a word like "PROOF").

Image files can be encrypted to prevent access by unauthorized users. The encryption scheme enables photographers to provide a code number to their customers once the right to use a particular image has been granted. The user then can put the Pro disc in a CD-ROM drive and enter the code number to free the image for use. Encryption also allows Pro Photo CD discs to be used for storing confidential images.

Professional photographers can also protect their work by distributing images for review on Kodak Photo CD Catalog discs, which store only low-resolution images.

Other supporting features that can be added to Pro Photo CD include the ability to adjust each scan to achieve desired results, and the ability to employ different "film terms" for retaining the subtle differences in professional film brands.

Using Photo CDs With a Computer

With appropriate software, users of desktop or other computer systems, including minicomputers and mainframes, can display and manipulate Photo CD images for use in a variety of applications.

To use Photo CD images, a computer system must have a CD-ROM XA disc drive and appropriate operating system support. The drive and system must be able to read hybrid discs and the sectors. The standards are specified by Sony/Philips in the Recordable Compact Disc Systems *Orange Book*. For more on CD-ROM standards and the various options CD-ROM, see Chapter Seven.

Multi-Session Drives

The first generation of CD-ROM XA drives were designed to play CDs that were recorded in a single session. Photo CD discs, however, were designed to record data in several sessions so that more than one roll of film can be stored on the disc. The older CD-ROM drives can only read the initial session on a multi-session disc, but more recent CD-ROM XA drives are able to read the multi-session discs. Sony's CDU-31A and CDU-561, Philips' CDD-461 and CDD-462, and Toshiba's third generation CD-ROM drives can read multi-session CD discs.

The Pioneer DRM-604X CD-ROM Minichanger is Photo CD compatible and allows users to access up to six CD-ROM discs in a single cartridge with an access time of 350 milliseconds, a very fast time for a disc changer.

The higher speed of transfer of Sony's CDU-561 SCSI drive, with a transfer rate of 330 kilobytes per second, will be appreciated by computer users of Photo CD. With slower drives, a Base resolution image might take 30 seconds or more to appear on screen, and it could take up to 15 minutes for a full-resolution 16 Base image to appear because the 24-bit color bitmap consists of 20 to 25 megabytes of data (Figure 2-17).

Figure 2-17. File sizes for each of the five Photo CD resolutions.

Image Type	Pixels	8-bit size	24-bit size (IBM)	24-bit size (Macintosh)
Base/16	192x128	25K	74K	99K
Base/4	384x256	99K	295K	394K
Base	768x512	394K	1.2MB	1.6MB
4Base	1536x1024	1.6MB	4.8MB	6.3MB
16Base	3072x2048	6.3MB	18.9MB	25.2MB

In addition to a compatible CD-ROM drive, the computer system must have a color monitor and color display adapter. Displays capable of showing 24-bit (16.7 million) color are recommended to provide the highest quality continuous-tone images. Because color images consume a great deal of file space, it is a good idea to have a large-capacity hard drive and a large amount of memory. It is not unusual for color-capable computer systems to have 16 MB of RAM or even more.

Software

Kodak has developed various software packages for computer use of Photo CD images. Kodak Photo CD Access includes functions for browsing, cut and paste, rotation, cropping, and export in a variety of formats. To use the images, software from other vendors must be capable of working with Photo CD directly or support file formats that can be exported from the Access software. Other Kodak software for Photo CD includes PhotoEdge for adjusting brightness, sharpness, contrast, and color balance; Renaissance for layout and design; and Shoebox image manager. These programs are described more extensively in Chapter Four.

An example of software support for Photo CD is the Apple QuickTime system software extensions (Figure 2-18). It is possible to directly access Photo CD images with Macintosh application software. Users click on a Photo CD icon to access thumbnail versions of images stored on Photo CD discs.

Storing Color and Tone Information

To store and convey color and tone information for each individual image pixel, an image-storing system must have a color-encoding scheme. Such a scheme can be based on the varying intensities of the three phosphors (red, green, and blue) in a cathode ray tube (CRT) or on the amount of ink or dye used to produce a print. Because the values that are stored for a particular image pixel depend on the characteristics of the display device, this type of encoding scheme is called device dependent. Kodak selected a device-independent color-encoding scheme, called PhotoYCC, for use in the Photo CD system.

Figure 2-18.
Macintosh users with Apple QuickTime installed can access thumbnail Photo CD images from the Finder.

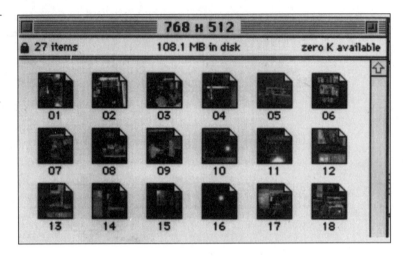

Today, most images are displayed and manipulated on a video-based device, even those destined for printing. Because quality and access time are major factors in video display, Kodak chose to base the PhotoYCC scheme on video standards established by international organizations. Technically, it is based on aspects of CCIR Recommendation 601-1 and also on the international recommendation for high-definition television production and exchange, CCIR 709.

Consistent, high-quality image print reproductions from Photo CD discs are obtained by converting PhotoYCC color information into forms that are compatible with other print reproduction systems.

Photo CD Image Compression

If the entire bitmap had to be stored, a 2048-line by 3072-pixel, 24-bit color image would require 20 to 25 MB of storage space. The Photo CD player accesses data at a rate of 150 kilobytes/sec. At this rate, two minutes would be required to access an image. Kodak has developed an image coding scheme that compresses the data for a single color image to about 4.5 MB on the average.

The Photo CD System first decomposes, or transforms, the original image data into a sequence of image components with a hierarchy of increasing resolution. The Base image of 512 lines by 768 pixels is successively interpolated and corrected to form images of increased resolution. The residual data for the high-resolution images are compressed using lossy and lossless techniques. Lossy techniques result in a higher degree of compression, but with a loss in image data. Lossless techniques offer limited compression ratios, but do not sacrifice any image data.

The Base, Base/4, and Base/16 images are stored in uncompressed form. For these images, software applications do not require any complex decompression routines. The resulting access time for a full display of the Base image is satisfactory under most circumstances. Because of the nature of the image compression scheme, the 4 Base image component includes luma (or brightness) data only.

In technical terms, the Photo CD System compression scheme employs chroma (or color) subsampling. This technique takes advantage of the characteristics of human visual perception to reduce the amount of data without a significant loss in perceived visual quality. In each image component, except 4 Base, the luma channel is accompanied by two chroma channels that have been subsampled in the horizontal and vertical directions. Thus, only one value from each of the chroma channels is required for every four values from the luma channel.

Chroma subsampling reduces the size of a full-resolution image to 9 MB. An additional and significant reduction in size is achieved by decomposing the highest resolution image data, storing the 4 Base and 16 Base components as residuals, or the differences from pixels at the previous level of resolution (Figure 2-19).

The Photo CD System employs a form of quantization and Huffman encoding to compress these residual data. Systems that support 4 Base and 16 Base resolutions are equipped to decode these residuals. The Photo CD compression scheme enables software to perform decompression easily. It also allows image recomposition to occur in the display buffer, minimizing the need for additional storage allocation (Figure 2-20).

To recompose an image for display at a resolution of 1024 lines by 1536 pixels, the image recomposition scheme interpolates the 512-line by 768-pixel luma Base image to a 1024-line by 1536-pixel image.

A 1024-line by 1536-pixel 4 Base residual is then decompressed from its Huffman-encoded form, and its elements are added to each corresponding pixel. The resulting image contains detail for the full 1024-line by 1536-pixel sampled image . To recompose an image to a resolution of 2048 lines by 3072 pixels, the process is essentially repeated, using a 16 Base residual. In this case, the process must be applied to the chroma channels, as well as to the luma channel.

Sound on a Photo CD Disc

The Photo CD file format supports two types of sound: CD-DA and interleaved audio. CD-DA is Compact Disc-Digital Audio, as defined by the Sony/Philips Red Book. It is the

Figure 2-19.
Decomposition of the luminance channel.

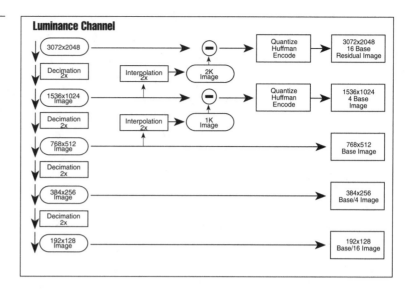

Figure 2-20.
Decomposition of the chrominance channel.

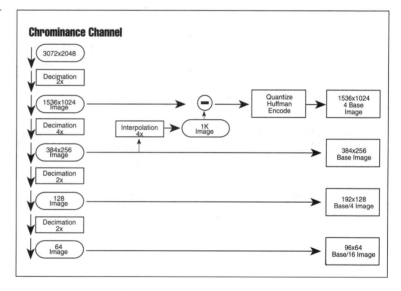

high-fidelity sound used on consumer audio compact discs. CD-DA sound fills the entire bandwidth of a CD-ROM drive, so it produces sound captions—sound that is connected to discrete images. CD-DA is used when high-fidelity, uncompressed sound is recorded.

With interleaved audio, pieces of sound are joined together to form continuous music, speech, or sounds. The sound is compressed through ADPCM (Adaptive Pulse Code Modulation) compression, the format defined in the Sony/Philips Yellow Book (CD-ROM XA). Compressed audio does not require the full bandwidth of the CD, and users can therefore play sound before, during, and after an image is displayed. The sound can be played as background music accompanying a digital photo album or a business presentation.

Photo CD discs with sound can carry up to 800 images recorded at Base resolution (television resolution). Discs recorded without images can carry up to 72 minutes of CD-DA sound or eight hours of stereo ADPCM sound.

These sound functions, combined with text and graphics, allow the presentation of interactive programs using Photo CD discs. It is expected that publishers will be able to produce pre-recorded Photo CD discs, and Photo CD service bureaus will be able to create custom Photo CD Portfolio discs for customers.

Photo CD Access Developer Toolkit

The Kodak Photo CD Access developer toolkit lets developers of computer software add Photo CD images to existing applications and to develop new applications featuring Photo CD imaging capability.

The Access developer toolkit includes a library of C language functions to read images from the Photo CD disc into memory, to expand the compressed image files and convert them into standard formats, and to provide basic image-manipulation capability for the image files.

Included with the toolkit are functions to build a flexible interface between applications and the Photo CD disc. The software automatically manages expansion of compressed image files and conversion to standard formats.

Control of image attributes such as orientation, resolution, color format, and area displayed is allowed. These include rotation from 0 to 270 degrees in 90 degree increments, mirror, flip, zoom, crop, and clipboard functions. The Kodak PhotoYCC color-encoding scheme is used to reduce storage requirements. PhotoYCC is easily transformed to other formats.

Image files on the Photo CD disc can be accessed at a variety of resolutions. The developer can select the appropriate resolution for a particular purpose. A read function in the toolkit adds a sixth resolution level by converting the Base/16 image to Base/64 as it is read into memory.

Images can be exported in the following standard formats for Microsoft Windows systems—EPS, TIFF, RIFF, PCX, and BMP (DIB). For Apple Macintosh systems images can be exported as EPS, TIFF, and PICT.

Photo Industry Support of Photo CD

Figure 2-21. A Fujix Photo CD.

Major photo manufacturers have announced their support of Photo CD. Fuji Photo Film will provide Photo CD transfer services in Japan, as well as workstation equipment for transferring both 35mm film and larger sizes in their Photo CD Workstation F-45 (Figures 2-21 and 2-22).

Figure 2-22.
Schematic drawing of Fujix F-45 Imaging Workstation.

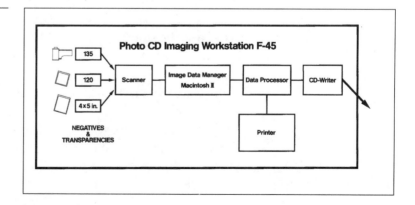

Figure 2-23. The Polaroid CS-500 Photo Scanner which will be used for print scanning on the Photo CD workstation.

Agfa-Gevaert, Europe's leading photo manufacturer, will use Photo CD discs as an additional source of input for the Agfa Digital Print System. Agfa views the Photo CD system as a bridge from film to electronic imaging.

Polaroid is another photo company that has endorsed the Photo CD standard for digitizing and displaying photographic images. Polaroid supplies a digital photo scanner to Kodak that digitizes prints up to 4 by 6 inches for storage on Photo CD discs (Figure 2-23).

How Photo CDs Are Manufactured

Compared to audio CDs or CD-ROMs, there are significant differences in the manufacture of Photo CDs. A continuous groove, with a slight wobble, is cut in the photoresist layer. Program information is recorded in this groove on the completed disc.

The groove is wobbled with a base frequency of 22.05 KHz. This base frequency is annotated with an absolute time in pregroove (ATIP) that is FM modulated and contains the parameters used to specify the time and the recommended optimum recording power. The ATIP is also used to control spindle speed.

A Photo CD disc contains a transparent substrate, a dye layer, a gold reflective layer, and a protective layer. A laser in the disc writer removes dye in specific areas to make pits that expose the underlying gold layer, which reflects more light than the dye layer when the disc is read.

A Photo CD disc is manufactured without recorded data on it. It may also be considered a write-once, read-many (WORM) times CD disc. Program information and image files are recorded on the disc by a laser that makes pits in the recording layer in the groove.

The high tolerances of manufacture and the materials used assure a long life for the recorded Photo CD disc (see Figure 2-24 in the color insert). Some estimates are that the disc will last 100 years or more. Only time will tell if this holds true, but the manufacturing process and the materials used are selected to achieve this longevity.

Figure 2-35. Kodak Photo CDs are manufactured under extremely rigid clean room conditions.

Family Portraits on Disc

APPLICATION BRIEF

The story of a growing granddaughter. (Photo by author from Photo CD)

Professional photographers can use the multi-session capability of Photo CD to record successive portraits of children as they grow on a single disc. With six photos per yearly sitting, the Photo CD allows 12 years of portraits to be put on a disc. Similarly, family portraits can be kept on a single disc to provide a continuing family record. The Photo CD discs are easily reproduced, so all family members can be given their own discs.

Professional photographers also can create Photo CD albums of family events such as weddings, anniversaries, and graduations. Sound and pictures can be part of a Portfolio disc made for each family member. A wedding Photo CD album, showing the wedding preparations as well as the event itself, can be coupled with a continuous audio track with music.

Bringing Real Estate Listings into the Digital Age

**APPLICATION
BRIEF**

Real estate agents can put pictures of homes for sale, both exterior and interior views, on Photo CD discs. Clients can then view selected property listings on TV and computer screens in the agency office or in the comfort of their own homes. When buyers find an interesting property, using Photo CD's branching feature, they can choose to view a series of exterior and interior pictures of the house and yard. The branching feature of Photo CD can also be used to select listed properties by categories such as price, style, and location.

For the real estate agent, Photo CD offers convenient storage and fast retrieval. Hundreds of properties, along with text and voice descriptions, can be put on a single Photo CD catalog or Portfolio disc. Color prints of selected properties can be quickly made by a color printer in the office.

Homes & Land Publishing Corp., which has more than 300 magazines in print or under contract in 45 states, has purchased the Kodak Photo CD Imaging Workstation 2400 to create Photo CD discs. The company imports the high-

Typical home real estate photo printed from a Photo CD image on a Kodak 7720 printer. (Courtesy Jukka Ropponen)

resolution images on the Photo CD disc directly into the pages of its Homes & Land *magazines. Over 700,000 real estate photos are taken annually for use in* Homes & Land *magazines. The photos used at* Homes & Land's *Tallahassee, FL, headquarters will be stored on Photo CD discs. The listings on the Photo CD disc will also be placed on the Kodak Picture Exchange network, making* Homes & Land *the first participant in a national real estate image network.*

With a color desktop computer and Kodak Picture Exchange, real estate agents can have immediate access to color photos of houses and properties listed in Homes & Land *magazines on a local as well as a national basis.*

Another real estate application of Photo CD is putting local MLS real estate listings and photographs on Photo CD discs. Several thousand homes can be put on a single Photo CD catalog disc.

Genealogy Record and Family History

APPLICATION BRIEF

A sample of a genealogy program produced on a Photo CD disc. (Permission to reproduce courtesy Eastman Kodak Company)

Family trees illustrated with photographs and drawings are well-suited for storage on Photo CD. Photographs can be integrated with the branches of the family tree. The branching feature of Photo CD will enable viewers to follow different family lines on the same disc. On Portfolio discs, voices as well as photographs can be included. The family tree CD is easily replicated so each family member can have a copy. The Photo CD disc can be added to a written family history as an insert.

On Photo CD discs, photographs of grandfathers and great-grandmothers retain their quality, unlike silver-halide prints or slides that deteriorate over time. Using a computer and imaging software, images on the disc can be used to create a composite image "family portrait," which combines generations that did not actually co-exist, for example, from great-great grandparents to the youngest generation.

Out of the Shoebox and Onto the CD Shelf

APPLICATION BRIEF

For many people, once slides and photographs come back from the developer and are looked at a few times, they go into a shoebox or bottom drawer for storage and are seldom seen again. Photo CD offers an easier and more convenient way to store the snapshot images and it provides a permanent medium that can replace mounds of slides, prints, and negatives. If the original slide or negative is lost, the Photo CD digital image can be used to make a new transparency or print with a quality that rivals the original.

Traditional photo albums are bulky and difficult to store. A single Photo CD can actually become several albums in one by setting up different sequences for viewing the images, for example, grandma's visit and Junior's 5th birthday can co-exist on the same disc.

Photo albums are a special family resource and sometimes are lent out and lost or never returned. By using Photo CD for family albums, individual images can easily be printed out to fill requests or the entire album can be duplicated for a family member.

A family enjoying Photo CD. (Permission to reproduce courtesy Eastman Kodak Company)

Photo CD as a Teaching Tool

APPLICATION BRIEF

A chart slide as one might be used in a classroom. (Permission to reproduce courtesy Eastman Kodak Company)

Teachers can use the selection and branching feature of Photo CD to display a series of images as they teach. Images can be shown on classroom TV sets or can be projected onto a screen. The teacher can even interrupt a sequence to show some additional illustrations on a specific topic, and then return to the sequence. Photo CD images can not only be displayed, but students may also include copies of the images in reports. A teacher can print out drawings and photographs on the discs to provide handouts or notes.

For elementary classes, photo images and audio are more interesting to the students than text and can enhance learning in subjects such as geography, history, and science. Film strips and 35mm sildes are commonly used as classroom teaching tools. In addition to displaying Photo CD images on TV screens, teachers can use liquid-crystal video projectors to display digital images on a screen.

Books on Photo CD—The Future Coffeetable Book?

APPLICATION BRIEF

From Alice to Ocean includes a Photo CD. (© 1992 Rick Smolan/ Against All Odds)

Authors of "coffeetable" books with high-quality illustrations are already including a Photo CD with their books. The reader not only gets more color images, but images that can be viewed on a home TV set. Photo CD discs also can bring the sounds and voices of the book to the reader.

Rick Smolan, author of the photographic A Day in the Life of... *book series, has put a Kodak Photo CD Portfolio disc in his new book,* From Alice to Ocean: Alone Across the Outback, *which documents the story of a woman's journey across the Australian outback. Smolan said that the disc contains photos, narration, and ambient sound that could not be included in the book itself. The images printed in the book also came from digital images on a Photo CD disc. Published by Addison Wesley,* From Alice to Ocean *was the first book to be made from Photo CD scanned images.*

Yearbooks on Photo CD Discs

APPLICATION BRIEF

Photo CD Portfolio discs offer a new way to publish school and college yearbooks. Combining sound and graphics with pictures will create a multimedia yearbook on a CD. The high school yearbook is one of the first candidates for conversion from printed books to CDs that can be viewed on the home TV. With the addition of voices, the Photo CD yearbooks will help keep high school memories alive and provide a keepsake that goes beyond the printed yearbook.

Another way to use Photo CDs in yearbook production is to have all the photographs taken at a school put on Photo CD discs. The digitized images on the discs can then be used instead of the original photographs to produce printed yearbooks.

Josten's Inc., the largest publisher of school yearbooks in the U.S., plans to use pictures written to Photo CDs as a way of taking images made in schools and bringing them directly into page make-up systems for the creation of photo yearbooks. In addition, this also opens the opportunity of creating Photo CD yearbooks as a supplement to printed yearbooks, or adding a Photo CD disc to the printed yearbook.

Students at work on a high school annual. (Permission to reproduce courtesy Eastman Kodak Company)

Manager of Josten's graphic systems research Dick Ruddy stated, "Josten's is excited about Kodak Photo CD because it brings a lot of opportunities to the yearbook creator. The young people in the schools who create the yearbooks have been asking for several years how they can get photos into their pages digitally. I believe that Kodak Photo CD will provide an economical way for them to do that."

Insurance Documentation

APPLICATION BRIEF

Insurance agents and claims adjusters can use Photo CD to store photographs of insured property and / or damage to the property. The digital Photo CD images can be transmitted by modem on request to the claims processing department. The photographs can be taken with conventional 35mm cameras.

Businesses and homeowners can record photographs of the content of their offices and homes on a Photo CD disc, along with relevant documentation. Multiple copies of the disc can be made inexpensively and stored in different locations. These discs can serve as an accurate record of contents in the event of a major loss through fire or a natural disaster.

Evaluating an automobile for insurance purposes. (Permission to reproduce courtesy Eastman Kodak Company)

Capturing Events on Portfolio Discs

APPLICATION BRIEF

There are numerous civic and sporting events that lend themselves to being captured on Photo CD. Almost any civic event—celebrations, festivals, fairs, conventions, homecomings, sports days, and parades—can be put onto Photo CD discs that combine photographs and sounds.

Sponsoring groups and participants are potential buyers of the civic event Portfolio discs, and copies can be put into local libraries or stored in city hall.

These civic event discs can be produced locally, using local photographic talent and a local photofinisher with a Photo CD workstation. Once the initial Portfolio disc is created, additional copies can be made by the photofinisher.

Photo CD can be useful for capturing sporting and civic events. (Photo by John R. Melson from Photo CD)

CHAPTER 3

Printing Photo CD Images

Once you have digital images on Photo CD discs, how do you go about making prints and slides from them? The day has not yet arrived when everyone is satisfied with viewing images solely on a screen. Color images on paper or projected from transparencies are still principal forms of communication at home and in business.

Photo CD, with its wide range of image formats, offers attractive possibilities for printing full-color images on paper or film. Thanks to the digital nature of Photo CD, you can use a computer to produce full-color copies of images on inkjet printers, color laser copier-printers, continuous-tone thermal dye-transfer printers, and other output devices.

But what are the advantages of using digital images stored on Photo CD discs instead of the original slides or prints? First, Photo CD discs are easier to store than film or prints. You do not need a darkroom and chemicals to make a color print or a slide from an image on Photo CD. For publishers, the biggest advantage may be that the color images on Photo CD discs are already digitized, which means they are ready for use in a computer. Starting with a digitized image eliminates a time-consuming step in the production process—sending the slides and photographs to a service bureau for scanning, or in the case of many desktop publishers, digitizing them on a color scanner linked to a computer.

Once an image has been digitized, a computer can be used to enhance the sharpness and colors of the image. You can enlarge or crop the image, or change or remove selected parts, such as telephone or power lines. If no modifications are desired, the computer can direct the digital image data to the output device of your choice.

To work with images from a Photo CD disc, a computer must have a compatible CD-ROM disc drive and image processing software. The imaging software is used to operate the CD-ROM drive, control a scanner, and send data to output devices such as color printers.

Many computer users do not have a color printer that will give them photo-quality color prints or films. Instead of making a major investment in a color printer, it is posssible to send discs to service bureaus that can produce high-quality prints or film from Photo CD images. They also can make prints or slides of images that have been modified or incorporated into a page layout program on a computer. Photofinishers who produce Photo CD discs are usually equipped with Kodak thermal dye-transfer printers as part of their PIW workstations. These printers can be used to make color prints up to 8 by 10 inches from images on Photo CD discs.

Thermal dye transfer printers produce continuous-tone color prints that look like photographic prints. The drawback is their high purchase cost and cost of consumables (dye sheets and special paper). Other color printers are less expensive and can print on ordinary white copier paper, but they do not produce photograph-like prints. The least expensive color printers are the thermal wax printers and color inkjet printers. Their output is suitable for use in documents and presentations.

Figure 3-1. The Xerox 5775 color laser printer.

Another option is to output the digital image on a color laser printer (Figure 3-1). A new generation of color photocopiers can also be used as scanners and printers. The color laser

PRINTING PHOTO CD IMAGES

Advertising Showcase

APPLICATION BRIEF

Photo CDs will allow advertising agencies to create customized showcases of their work for presentation to prospective clients. The high-quality color images can be shown on a TV set or projected onto a screen. During discussions, specific advertisements can be retrieved from Photo CD discs and used to illustrate a point.

During ad creation, clients can be shown images from Photo CD discs for approval. These same images can be used for the creation of ad "comps" and for the final production of ads because of the high resolution capability of Photo CD images.

Photo CD discs can also allow agencies to more easily search through and view available photos from photo stockhouses and individual photographer portfolios. Thumbnail resolution images can be used in preparing ad concepts. For special photographs, ad agencies can use the Kodak Picture Exchange network to search image databases throughout the world.

Joe Darby, president of The Graphics Group sees, "The Photo CD system gives us new opportunities that we haven't had before. We'll be able to move into multimedia, and we'll be able to move into presentation graphics. Although we're into them now, we're not nearly as expansive as we are going to be in the very near future.

"It's a great storage medium. The customer can have all of the pictures of their catalog on a CD disc. They can review it at the shop in their location. It gives them a great amount of flexibility, to be able to work back and forth with this and to make color corrections and color adjustments...all starting from a Photo CD base."

printer and the color copier-printer both use the electro-photographic technology pioneered by Xerox. Color prints made on these output devices can approach the quality of images printed on a four-color press.

Finally, the digital image can be returned to silver-based film and paper. There are many printers and film recorders that can make prints, transparencies, or negatives from digital images. These printers complete the cycle that begins with a camera, film, and Photo CD. With Photo CD, we go from silver to silicon, and with photographic printers, we go from silicon to silver.

Color Management of Digital Images

One of the great advantages of the Photo CD is the color uniformity of the images stored on the disc. At the time of scanning, a standard set of algorithms is used to match the colors to images viewed on TV screens. Color continuity is maintained from image to image. Much of this knowledge in color continuity comes from Kodak's experience in traditional photography.

The Base image format is designed primarily to produce good images on TV and computer screens. But producing good-looking prints is not so simple. There is a wide variation in the technologies used to produce color prints, and each of these technologies handles color a little differently. There are even variations among printers that use the same technology. For example, one thermal-transfer printer may use ribbons of cyan, yellow, and magenta to produce prints, while another may use cyan, yellow, magenta, and black.

One solution to this problem is color management software. This software, available from several vendors, ensures that the colors on screen will be accurately reproduced when the image is printed on paper. Without a color management system, the tones and color in the reproduced image may not match either the original scene or the image on a TV or computer screen.

Color Gamuts

Not all the colors seen on screen can be reproduced on paper, and conversely not all the printable colors can be reproduced exactly on the screen. What color management software provides is consistent color throughout the entire system, from the input scanner to the color display to the output devices and finally to the printing press.

Color management packages take varying approaches to the task, but the general idea is to store information about the color reproduction characteristics of specific displays, input devices, and/or output devices in what's known as a "device profile." Each profile describes the range of colors (known as the "color gamut") that can be reproduced by a particular model of a particular printer, scanner, or display. The profile also accounts for any tendency the device has to distort colors. When the image is printed or displayed, the software automatically modifies it to accommodate the capabilities of that particular device.

Kodak ColorSense Color Manager

Some color management packages are specific to certain printers, scanners, or displays. They are generally sold by peripheral manufacturers to ensure better color reproduction. But other color management products are designed to tie together all of the hardware peripherals used in a computer system. One such product is Kodak's ColorSense Color Manager. Other color management products are described in Chapter Four.

The Kodak ColorSense color manager is a software package that maintains consistent color in a computer system from input to output. ColorSense is used to calibrate the computer display to show accurate repeatable colors and to preview how the on-screen colors will look when printed.

Because individual displays vary, even if they are the same make and model, a monitor calibrator and calibration software is required to automatically correct the color characteristics of the screen. For improved viewing, the screen is blackened around the edges.

Generally, computer displays are able to show a broader range of colors than a printer can produce. To avoid wasting printing time and materials, ColorSense has the ability to "preview" on the screen how the file will appear when printed with a particular printer. The color characteristics of several printers can be stored in the computer. The "preview" allows proofing changes to be made before actually producing any hardcopy.

The complex color technology required to do this is hidden beneath an easy-to-use interface. The ColorSense user chooses the devices (scanners, monitors, printers) that will be used and the color manager software does the rest. ColorSense directly supports Photo CD files (Figure 3-2).

The operator can zoom in and out of the displayed image when editing it. ColorSense can modify colors and convert between color spaces. Thumbnails are displayed when

Figure 3-2. The Kodak ColorSense Color Management System provides WYSIWYG color.

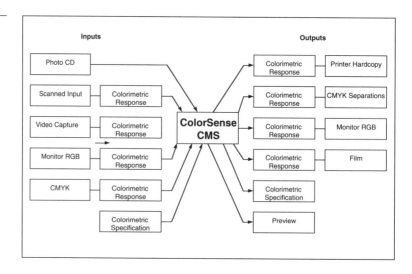

opening files and automatic color management is possible by configuring default devices.

Device Color Profiles (DCPs) included in ColorSense describe the specific color characteristics of widely used printers, scanners, and monitors. During the installation program, these DCPs are placed in the appropriate folders and can be read automatically by ColorSense. Even output to different paper types are included in the DCPs.

DCPs apply to all platforms, and color corrections are preserved when files are transferred across platforms. Colors created on the Macintosh are automatically displayed with the correct colors in Windows on a PC or on a Sun computer.

Targets

Scanner characteristics also vary from unit to unit, so a scanner target and calibration software is also included for automatic correction of the scanner's color characteristics. The target is a reference image that has been scanned and measured by the developer. When the target is scanned by the calibration software, the software compares the scanned color values with the known values from the developer's scan. The software can then modify future scans to ensure better accuracy. Whether you use a reflection or film scanner, the calibration software compensates to produce color matches on the computer display.

A system extensions component allows color management to be applied to files open in other applications. This adds functionality by providing color-managed print preview and printing output capability within applications such as QuarkXPress, Aldus Persuasion, and Adobe Illustrator.

Because different scanners, displays, and printers have different ranges of colors that they are able to print, ColorSense uses gamut compression schemes to create equivalent colors from device to device.

The goal of ColorSense is to provide accurate and predictable color. The professional using digital color photographs wants to be sure that the color seen on the screen will be the color in the end product.

PostScript

One of the key elements in many printers is a "page description language" from Adobe Systems known as PostScript. PostScript is a computer language, but unlike general-purpose computer languages, it has one main function: to produce images in the form of dots on a printer, imagesetter, or other output device. It uses English-like commands that can create almost any kind of graphic image or text.

It is possible to write a PostScript program to produce pages with the most complex graphics. This is not very practical because writing PostScript programs requires considerable training and skill. However, most computer programs—especially graphics programs—have the ability to generate PostScript files.

Adobe licenses PostScript to manufacturers of printers and imagesetters, who incorporate the technology into their products. When you print a file on a PostScript printer or imagesetter, your software generates a PostScript program and sends it to the output device. There, a controller or raster-image processor (RIP) converts the commands in the PostScript program into instructions that guide the printer as it produces the page.

One advantage of PostScript is device-independence. A file that prints on one PostScript device can be printed with little or no modification on another PostScript device. PostScript also offers special features for handling the printing of text and graphics, especially color graphics.

The original version of PostScript had some limitations in its ability to produce color images. However, Adobe has released a revision of the language called PostScript Level 2 that overcomes most of these limitations. Many of the functions of PostScript 2 relate to such issues as color calibration. Like the color management systems available from Kodak and other vendors, it supports the use of device profiles that account for the color reproduction characteristics of specific printers. The idea is to make the printed page match as closely as possible the original image.

Not all printers used for reproduction of photographs are PostScript devices. But because of PostScript's device-independence and powerful graphics features, many computer graphics users—especially Macintosh users—require PostScript compatibility in their printers.

Because PostScript is so popular, several developers have created PostScript "clones" that emulate PostScript. A printer equipped with a PostScript clone controller can theoretically print the same files as an Adobe-licensed printer.

Prints from Photo CD

There are five major technologies for direct printing of color digital images: thermal wax, thermal dye transfer (also known as dye sublimation), inkjet, electrophotography/electrostatic, and silver halide. Each has advantages and disadvantages. An additional option is to produce color separations on a PostScript imagesetter for use on an offset press. This is discussed in Chapter Five.

Until recently, the major disadvantage was the high cost of printers that could produce high-quality color prints. Advances in the technologies and competitive pricing are bringing costs down.

Many factors are involved in producing photographic-quality prints. The tone reproduction of an image depends to a great extent on the image content. The reproduction challenge becomes greater with images that have large amounts of subtle detail.

When working with imaging software, adjustments can be made to highlights and shadows to move them closer to the midtone range. Gray-scale and color balance can be automatically adjusted by color management or image-editing software. This is what makes a difference in the ultimate quality of prints produced from a digital image.

Prints produced by color output devices fall into one of two categories: halftones and continuous tones. A halftone is an image composed of dots. In a conventional printed halftone, the size of the dots determines the relative lightness or darkness of different areas in the image. Most printers cannot produce variable-sized dots, so they use a process called "dithering" to get a similar effect. In dithering, the printer produces dots in variable-sized clusters known as halftone "cells" that are equivalent to the dots seen in traditional halftones.

Traditional silver-halide photographic prints are continuous-tone images. Instead of being composed of variable-sized dots, they are composed of tiny particles, each of which can reproduce a wide range of colors and tints. Thermal dye transfer, silver-halide, and some inkjet printers are capable of producing continuous-tone prints.

As a rule of thumb, the human visual system, at normal viewing distances, is satisfied with images that exceed 254 dots per inch. When the resolution falls below that level, artifacts may become visible. Some color printers produce prints in which the dot pattern is very noticeable.

Even with color management software, the "equivalent" colors produced by the different types of printers will not always look the same because of the inherent differences in the inks and the processes. What color management software can do is provide a consistent relationship between devices, so that a particular shade of red from one printer can be used to predict what another output device will produce. But the most important advantage of color matching is that it gives the user a way of predicting what the colors and image will look like when it comes off the press.

Thermal Wax Printers

In thermal wax printers, heat applied to color wax in a ribbon softens the wax and transfers it to paper. The thermal printhead has an array of pins that can be individually heated. Each pin is heated to same degree, so each dot of color that is transferred to the paper is the same size and has the same intensity of color.

Because of the high color intensity of the colored wax, thermal transfer prints and transparencies have brilliant, saturated colors (Figure 3-3).

The thermal wax printer uses the primary subtractive colors—cyan, magenta, yellow, black—to produce color halftones. Each dot in the halftone is a single intensity of one of the four primary colors. Dithering algorithms calculate which dot of color goes where in each halftone cell. Each halftone cell is a square array of dots.

Halftoning reduces the perceived resolution of the image. A printer with a 300-dpi resolution may produce halftones with an effective resolution of only 50 lines per inch. It is the number of halftone cells and not the dots per inch that determine perceived resolution.

Figure 3-3. QMS offers two sizes of thermal wax printer.

Thermal wax printers are relatively inexpensive, compared to other color printers. Their output is excellent for overhead transparencies and when bright, saturated colors are wanted. The prints also can be used to proof for cropping, image enhancements, and modifications, but not for color balance because the color dots all are the same intensity and size. Text and images with lines reproduce well in thermal wax prints.

Thermal Dye Transfer Printers

Known by many names, thermal dye transfer, dye sublimation, or dye diffusion thermal transfer (D2T2), all of these names describe a technology that uses dye ribbons and a thermal head.

In a thermal dye transfer printer, the color's intensity is controlled by varying the heating of each pin in the printhead. This is different from the thermal wax process, where the heads are heated to the same degree for each dot printed, and each dot of color has the same intensity of color. By varying the intensity of each dot, the printer is capable of producing continuous-tone images (Figure 3-4).

The high-resolution thermal print head transfers dye from a special three-color (cyan/magenta/yellow) or four-color (cyan/magenta/yellow/black) ribbon to the paper or film.

Figure 3-4. The Kodak 7700 was one of the first thermal dye transfer printers on the market.

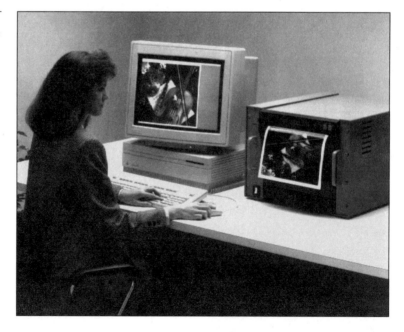

One color at a time is printed, which means that three or four passes are needed for each print.

Specially coated material is required for the thermal dye transfer printer. The paper is generally a photographic grade with a plastic coating on the top and bottom to provide a smooth surface. Some thermal dye transfer printers require a plastic sheet with no paper component.

Photographic-quality film material is used to make transparencies. The flatness and thickness of this transparency material is critical because the spacing between the printing head and the material must be constant. This means, in many cases, that the paper or film of one manufacturer may not work in another manufacturer's printer.

Thermal dye transfer printers generally have a large frame buffer that allows for the storage of single or multiple images. In many of the printers being made today, digital signal processing technology is used for color and image enhancement as well as scaling.

If you look across most thermal dye transfer prints, they look much like a conventional photographic print. They do not have a raised ink surface that creates an embossed effect. However, text, fine lines, and images with sharp edges may not be optimally reproduced in these prints and transparencies. Thermal dye transfer printers also have limitations as color proofing devices for prepress operations because they cannot reproduce the dots used in offset lithography.

It is possible to produce excellent overhead film transparencies on thermal dye traansfer printers. Special dye materials have been developed that produce very intense images suitable for projection. Dye sub film images also are being used as negatives for making photographs in the conventional way.

Figure 3-5. The Sony CVP-G 500 printer prints snapshot-sized thermal dye transfer prints.

Thermal dye transfer printers are available with resolutions of 200, 300, and 400 dots per inch. They can produce prints ranging in sizes from 3.5 by 5 inches (Figure 3-5) to 11 by 17 inches.

Inkjet Printers

There are two basic type of inkjet printers: drop-on-demand ink, and continuous-stream ink. The drop-on-demand inkjet, also called a thermal inkjet, uses a piezoelectric transducer to create a droplet of ink (Figure 3-6). An electronic signal triggers the transducer to eject a droplet of ink from the printhead. Canon has developed a bubble jet that uses a pulsed heating element to create a gas bubble that ejects the ink droplet. Separate printheads are needed for each color of ink used in an inkjet printer. The pulse that forms the ink droplet can be varied enough to create larger or smaller droplets, which can be used to create a gray-scale image.

Most desktop color inkjet printers lack the color saturation capability to produce photo-quality images. However, these

Figure 3-6. The drop-on-demand ink jet uses a piezoelectric element to create pressure.

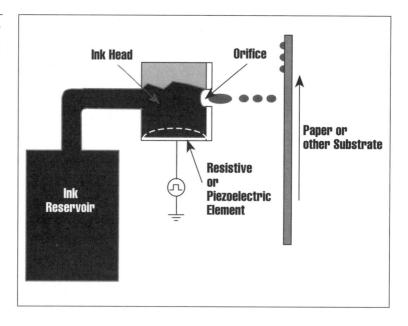

inkjet printers are relatively inexpensive and can be used to make positioning and cropping proofs.

The continuous inkjet, often referred to as the Hertz or Type 1 inkjet, sends a stream of charged and uncharged ink droplets toward the paper. As the droplets pass through an electric field, the charged droplets are deflected away and the uncharged droplets continue on a straight path toward the paper (Figure 3-7).

Figure 3-7. The formation of droplets in a Type I inkjet are determined by the speed of the droplet and the nozzle's diameter.

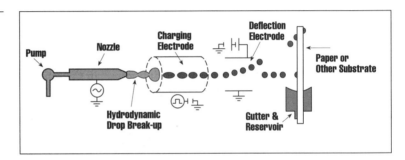

The four primary colors (CMYK) can be placed on a paper at one time. Since the continuous inkjet is a non-contact process, a variety of papers as well as large-format sizes can be used. This type of inkjet can print on almost any substrate—paper, film, cardboard, and even textiles.

The Iris inkjet sold by Scitex is widely used by newspapers and service bureaus for proofing on the same paper that will be used on the press (Figure 3-8). An inkjet printer developed by Stork also uses Hertz technology. Both the Iris and Stork inkjets are capable of producing nearly photographic-quality prints.

Figure 3-8. The Iris SmartJet is a Type I inkjet printer.

Electrophotographic Printers
Color copiers with computer interfaces have been introduced by Canon, Kodak, Xerox, and others. The copier terminology is somewhat misleading because some of

these devices also serve as scanners to digitize images and as printers that can output directly from computer files.

The Canon Color Laser Copier 500 was one of the first full-color copier-printers to reach the market (Figure 3-9). With its associated electronic interfaces, the CLC 500 can output color pages directly from computer files. It has a resolution of 400 dots per inch and can produce print-quality images on standard copier paper.

The CLC 500 has been installed in a number of quick print shops and is finding increasing use in large companies. While the printing is limited to one side, the cyan, magenta, yellow, and black toners provide an excellent quality image.

Some companies offer interface products for the CLC 500 that improve the quality of printed images in addition to providing a computer interface. The most well known of these is the Fiery controller from Electronics for Imaging (EFI), a company that has done much work to bring high-quality color to the desktop computer. The controller uses EFI's color management software for accurate color repro-

Figure 3-9. A cross-section of the Canon Color Laser Copier 500.

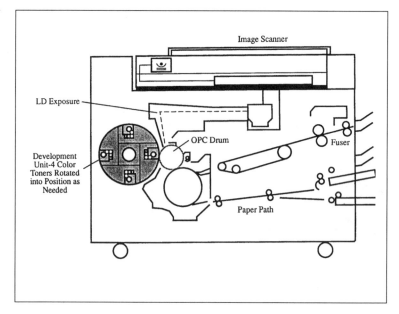

duction and also allows the copier to produce continuous-tone prints. It also uses a version of PostScript licensed from Adobe Systems, turning the CLC 500 into a PostScript printer.

Versions of the Fiery controller are also available for the Kodak 1550 ColorEdge copier (Figure 3-10), a special version of the CLC 500 custom manufactured for Kodak, and for the Xerox 5775 Printer, which can print on both sides of a page.

Electrophotographic copier-printers are quite expensive. Some service bureaus have begun using the Canon CLC with a Fiery controller as an "on-demand" printer. Another interface system used in the CLC is DiceNet (Digital Imaging Canon Equipment-Network). DiceNet allows the interface of multiple CLC 500s and Canon Bubble Jet printers. Networking can be to Macintosh, PC, Amiga, and UNIX computers.

Electrophotographic copier-printers can be used to produce multiple copies of pages in full color. The quality of the color reproduction is high, appoaching that of a printing press.

Figure 3-10. The EFI Fiery controller produces continuous-tone color images on the Kodak 1550 ColorEdge copier.

Silver Halide Printers

It is possible to return the digital image from silicon to silver. A number of printers are available that use photo-sensitive silver-halide film and paper as the receiving sheet. The output can be a transparency, film negative, or a photograph.

The Fujix Pictrography 3000 uses a donor and receiver, with the silver-halide donor transferring the color image to a receiver with the application of water and pressure.

The Ilford Digital Photo Imager uses liquid-crystal light-valve (LCLV) technology to project images on a conventional photographic media (Figure 3-11). Prints can be produced at a rate of up to 180 per hour.

The LVT (light valve technology) printer from Kodak (Figure 3-12) uses PLZT (lead, lanthanum, zirconate, titanate) light valve. Tungsten light is modulated by the PLZT crystal in order to write an image to conventional color negative film or paper. A high-resolution print can take several minutes to write.

Figure 3-12. The
Kodak LVT printer
produces output on
photographic film or
paper.

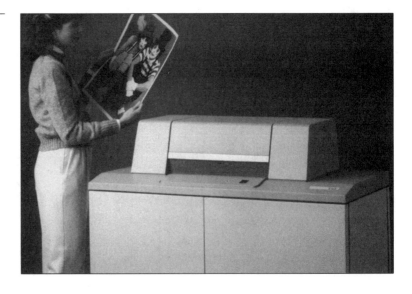

The 3M Color Laser Imager writes images on infrared-sensitive silver-halide color paper with three laser diodes. The Polaroid Digital Image Printer also uses LEDs (light-emitting diodes) to expose Spectra instant film.

The Agfa Digital Printing System can output Photo CD images on conventional color negative paper using a cathode-ray tube (CRT) writer. The system printed sizes up to 20 by 30 cm. (Figure 3-13).

Kodak has developed a CRT-based printer for producing the thumbnail image prints for Photo CD cases. This printer can produce enlargements up to 4 by 6 inches.

Film Recorders

More than a dozen film recorders are available for creating film images from digital images. Using high-resolution black-and-white CRTs, individual red, green, and blue exposures are made using color filters. Output film sizes can be from 35mm to 8 by 10 inches on color positive or color negative film. Resolutions range from 2000 lines per inch to 16,000 lines per inch. The Solitaire Image Recorder from Management Graphics can support up to 36 bits of color

Figure 3-13. The Agfa Digital Print System can output prints from Photo CDs.

Figure 3-14. The Solitaire 8 Professional film recorder has addressability up to 8192 by 8192 on 35mm film.

and can expose an 8 by 10-inch film at 16,000 lines per inch in three minutes or less (Figure 3-14).

There are a number of challenges in selecting a film recorder. Resolution is a key factor, but the spot size of the recording beam of the CRT also should be taken into consideration if high resolution is required. The ultimate measure is how many lines per millimeter can be recorded on the film. There is a concern also for smooth and accurate reproduction of colors. If there is not enough color depth, colors will begin to band, which is not acceptable in a photo image. The time it takes to record an image can create production bottleneck. Often this problem may be the software being used and not the film recorder.

Film recorders offer an inexpensive way to create a high-resolution negative or transparency of a Photo CD image. The negative can be used in an enlarger to produce a photograph. We have seen 40 by 60-inch enlargements of images from Photo CD with no noticeable loss of quality.

Large-Format Printing

Photo CD images have sufficient resolution to be used for making large color prints such as posters, wall displays, and billboards. In the past few years, software has been developed to handle the image files required for large-format output, and printer manufacturers are beginning to introduce large-format printers

Iris inkjet and Canon Bubble Jet were the first printers to be widely used by service bureaus and professional photo labs for making large prints from digital images. A new generation of large-format color electrostatic printer is being introduced. These printers can produce poster-width color prints up to several feet long.

Figure 3-15 The Calcomp 68000 GA large-format color electrostatic printer can print on 36 or 44-inch paper.

The 68000 series of electrostatic printers from Calcomp output color images at 2 inches per second on 36-inch or 44-inch rolls of paper. An optional PostScript controller is compatible with the Macintosh, DOS, Windows, and Unix operating environments (Figure 3-12). Other developers of large-format color printing systems include Cactus, Synergy, Colossal Graphics, and Visual Edge Technology.

Large-format printing from digital images is still in its early stage, and the full potential of this printing option has yet to be realized. Innovative applications such as "posters on demand" printing in stores, banners that combine text and pictures, wall hangings for conventions, backdrops for trade show displays, and sale signs for store windows could lead to the successful launch of new business enterprises.

Using Photo CD to Display Museum Collections in Kiosksv

APPLICATION BRIEF

Museum directors are excited about being able to use Photo CD to put pictures of collections on display in kiosks, which also could provide on-demand information to museum visitors. Museum collections that normally would not be seen can be photographed and the images stored on Photo CD discs for archival purposes. Catalog discs of museum collections of ceramics, textile, sculpture, paintings, and ancient artifacts could be sold to the general public in museum shops, bookstores, and by direct mail. Directors of several of the world's leading museums are planning to use Photo CDs in display kiosks and as a product that can be sold to the public.

One application is the use of Photo CD players and standard TV sets in kiosks as stand-alone units for providing information on-demand to museum patrons. Selections could include photo images of art works, maps, charts and narrated information. In addition to information kiosks, museums can set up viewing areas equipped with Photo CD players and television sets or computers that can be used to search through the museum's image database. Museum shops can offer Photo CDs with images of museum items for home or classroom use.

The director of the Getty art history information program, Dr. Michael Ester, spoke of the efficacy of the Kodak CD choice: "In choosing CD storage, Kodak has picked a nearly ubiquitous medium that is equally suitable for conventional television or for accessing images in a computer-controlled environment. For museums and archives, Photo CD offers inviting possibilities for reaching visitors and professional audiences and for storing image reproductions."

CHAPTER 4

Enhancing Photo CD Images

Once an image is available in Photo CD's digital format, much can be done both to enhance it and to create new interpretations. Enhancing or retouching a photograph is not new. For generations, newspapers had art departments for retouching photographs taken by staff photographers. The effort was not to alter the images, but to take out distracting backgrounds, to make faces more reproducible, and sometimes to join several images together for an artistic effect.

Today, image enhancement software makes it possible for images to be improved dramatically in quality. Users can also create a wide range of special effects using image filters and other functions found in these programs. It is even possible to create entirely new images from the original.

As with all tools, there is opportunity for misuse. Color copy machines produce excellent color reproductions, but as we found out in one city, high school students learned to copy U.S. currency on the machines. The power of computer image enhancement may tempt some to misuse copyright material. Photo CD offers ways to circumvent such misuse, or at least makes it possible to identify the original image buried within the altered version.

All image enhancement and modification is done on a computer, not on the Photo CD disc itself. A computer cannot alter the stored images on the Photo CD disc, and it does not store altered images on the Photo CD disc. The altered image files are stored in the computer's hard drive or an auxiliary storage device. Only with the Pro Photo CD Master format can images be written from a workstation back to a Photo CD disc. But even then, the original image cannot be altered.

To use Photo CD on a computer, you need a CD-ROM drive that can read Photo CD discs. Early versions of the CD-ROM XA drive were designed to read discs that had only a single session recorded on them, and these early XA drives can read only the first set of images on a multi-session Photo CD disc. The sessions recorded after the first cannot be accessed. Later XA drives can read both single-session and multi-session Photo CD discs.

Trade Show Kiosks

APPLICATION BRIEF

A kiosk with Photo CD player could allow trade show attendees to order products. (Courtesy Interad Corp.)

While it might be best to display the original product, at trade shows it may not possible to show a company's full line and printed catalogs are not very effective in that setting. At most trade shows, space limits the number and variety of products that can be shown. Kiosks incorporating Photo CD players and color television monitors can provide an answer, allowing customers to see and hear product information. Using Kodak Photo CD jukebox players, up to 10,000 images with sound can be stored in a single unit.

With Photo CD, continuous high-quality images can be part of a display booth. Photo CD can be use to display products on a TV or large projection screen, along with sound. A regular Photo CD player or a personal computer can be used to operate the product display, which can augment the "live" product demos in the booth.

Kodak Software

Photo CD images can be imported into image enhancement programs in one of two ways. Many software packages already have interfaces to Photo CD, and the list is growing all the time. These interfaces were created using the Photo CD Developers Kit, which Kodak provides to developers of graphics software. Software equipped with these interfaces can import Photo CD images directly from the disc. Because Apple's QuickTime (beginning with version 1.5) supports Photo CD, Macintosh users running QuickTime can open image files on Photo CD discs as if they were ordinary files on a hard drive.

Photo CD Access

If the software does not have an interface to Photo CD discs, Kodak's Photo CD Access is the answer (Figure 4-1). This software can convert Photo CD images to the most common image formats in use today. In addition to Access, Kodak has developed several other software packages that support Photo CD image handling and enhancements.

Figure 4-1. Kodak's Photo CD Access software can convert Photo CD images into image formats used in personal computers.

Figure 4-2. Using Photo CD Access to extract an image directly as a TIFF or other format file.

Photo CD Access is a low-cost tool designed for occasional users of Photo CD images and for those who want to import Photo CD images into such applications as Adobe Photoshop or Aldus PhotoStyler. It is available in versions for the Macintosh and Windows 3.x. It is sold directly by Kodak, but future plans call for the software to be bundled with CD-ROM drives and software packages marketed by other companies.

The Access software has familiar, menu-driven graphical interfaces that allow users to easily load and manipulate the photographic images stored on Photo CD discs. Users can perform basic functions such as cropping, zooming, and image rotation. Images can also be exported to word processing, desktop publishing, illustration, database, and presentation programs—any applications that support bit-mapped color or bi-tonal images (Figure 4-2). On the Macintosh, Access supports PICT, TIFF, and EPS file formats. Running under Windows, it supports BMP, EPS, PCX, RIFF, TIFF, and WMF formats.

Instead of using Kodak's technical terminology for the five image formats on a Photo CD disc, the Access software uses terms that are more familiar to consumers. The Base/16 image is called "Wallet," Base/4 "Snapshot," Base "Standard," 4 Base "Large," and 16 Base "Poster."

Users can access images at any of five supported resolutions, selecting a specific resolution based on how the image will be used. The thumbnail or wallet image is useful for image selection and previewing, while the snapshot is suited for low-resolution image manipulation. The base image, which is NTSC TV-compatible, provides moderate resolution. The large or HDTV image is for high-resolution image handling, and the poster image is for photographic-quality printing and enlarging.

Photo CD Access software features are available through easy-to-use pull-down menus. The first menu, File, gives

Figure 4-3. The crop window in Access allows you to select just the portion of an image that you want.

access to the photographic index or any image on a Photo CD disc, and also allows export of a selected image to a computer file. The Edit menu includes commands for cutting or copying all or part of an image to an electronic clipboard, from which it can be "pasted" into another application. The pasted image matches the resolution and cropping of the original image selection.

A special feature in the Windows version is the ability to import Photo CD images without leaving the current application by using Dynamic Data Exchange (DDE) macros. DDE is a technology in Windows that allows communication and data transfer among applications. Because the Access software is written to the DDE Windows standard, a DDE macro can be made for any application that will support it. This function is similar to Publish and Subscribe in Macintosh software.

Other options include Resolution, where you select and use images at any supported resolution or apply a resolution to one or more selected images. Palette displays image formats supported on the platform and allows you to choose among color, greyscale, or bi-tonal formats. A Palette selection can be applied to one or more selected images.

You can easily select just a portion of a desired image by using Access' cropping function. From the main window, you can drag the borders of the image in one of four directions to lick the area you want. Alternatively, you can select the Crop Window, which shows the cropping rectangle superimposed over the entire image (Figure 4-3). In either case, Access shows you how the file size of the image portion you have selcted. When you export a cropped image, only the cropped portion is saved to disk.

The Windows menu allows you to choose various options for viewing images, such as contact sheet, new photo, and others. You can use the Beveled Matte feature in Photo View to select and size a portion of the image. The Orientation option allows clockwise or counterclockwise rotation in 90-degree increments with horizontal or vertical flips. Orientation can be applied to one or more selected images. A Help menu gives you context-sensitive on-line help.

Other Kodak software packages intended for use with Photo CD include PhotoEdge, Shoebox, Browser, and Renaissance.

PhotoEdge

PhotoEdge is designed to meet the needs of the business user who is beginning to work with images on the desktop. Like Access, PhotoEdge lets a user zoom, crop, rotate, and flip Photo CD images. It also supports the same image file formats (Figure 4-4).

In addition, Kodak PhotoEdge software makes it possible to modify pictures that are under- or over-exposed or need sharpening. Users can also adjust contrast, color, or soft focus. The software is available in Macintosh and Windows formats.

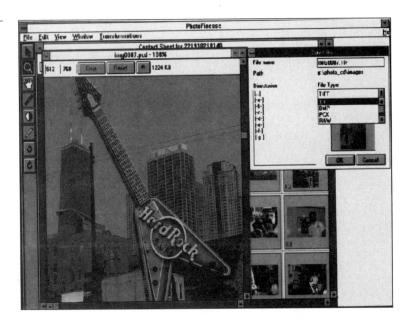

Figure 4-4. Kodak PhotoEdge software includes a number of image-editing functions.

ENHANCING PHOTO CD IMAGES

Shoebox

Shoebox, which is also available in Macintosh and Windows versions, helps automate the storage and retrieval of images for anyone maintaining a Photo CD image archive. Using Shoebox, users store lower-resolution thumbnail images in a database that resides on their hard drive or similar media.

Because of their relatively small file sizes, these images can be searched rapidly using keywords. For example, a designer sitting at a workstation could enter the words "football," "autumn," and "college" to locate thumbnails of homecoming games. Users can also browse through thumbnails in a Kodak Shoebox database.

Double-clicking on a thumbnail tells the software to retrieve the corresponding high-resolution image file from the proper Photo CD disc. (If the right disc isn't mounted in the CD-ROM XA drive, the software will prompt the user, identifying which disc to load.) The resulting images can be viewed in color or gray-scale and in a variety of sizes and resolutions. They can also be framed on the screen, cropped, or incorporated into an on-screen "slide show." Images can be exported as PICT or TIFF files to other applications. Future versions of Shoebox will allow users the option of linking to the Kodak Picture Exchange (See Chapter Eight) to enable searches of its vast image database.

Browser

Kodak Browser software, a scaled-down version of Shoebox, will be on every Kodak Photo CD Catalog disc. Browser is designed to give the casual user keyword access to images from the moment the Photo CD disc is inserted into a CD-ROM XA drive.

Renaissance

Kodak Renaissance is a Macintosh-based color design tool that has built-in support for Photo CD images. The program incorporates many of the page layout features found in programs like QuarkXPress along with graphics functions found in packages like Adobe Illustrator. With its ability to incorporate text, graphics, and photographs, it is aimed at graphic designers who want to produce ads and other design-intensive print pieces. It allows direct import of Photo CD images, as well as TIFF, PICT, and EPS files.

Software for Image Enhancement

For several years, graphics software developers have offered programs that allow manipulation and enhancement of photographic images. At first, these image-editing programs were intended for use with images captured by means of a desktop scanner or video digitizer. However, they are also ideal for manipulation of Photo CD images. Many have been upgraded to offer direct access to Photo CD discs, but any image-editing program can work with Photo CD images if it supports any of the file formats that can be exported from Access.

The first image-editing packages to see widespread use were ImageStudio, initially available from Letraset, and Digital Darkroom, originally developed by Silicon Beach Software. Both of these programs ran on the Macintosh and were limited to editing gray-scale images. However, they offered powerful features that allowed users to modify brightness, contrast, sharpness, and other image settings. Users could also create composite images using the programs' powerful cut-and-paste and cloning features.

ImageStudio is no longer available; Fractal Design, the company that originally developed the program for Letraset now offers a program called Sketcher that includes many of ImageStudio's functions. However, Digital Darkroom is still available from Aldus Corp., which acquired Silicon Beach Software several years ago.

ImageStudio and Digital Darkroom spawned a new category in computer graphics software that has since been joined by several packages that can manipulate color or gray-scale images. These programs include Adobe Photoshop and Fractal ColorStudio on the Macintosh, and Photoshop, Aldus PhotoStyler, Micrografx Picture Publisher, Halo Desktop Imager, Image-In Color and Professional, and ZSoft PhotoFinish on the PC.

Image-Editing Software Features

Although each package has its own unique features, a number of general functions are common to all.

Paint Tools
Almost all image-editing programs include painting tools that allow the user to retouch or add effects to an image. Typically, these tools include a standard paintbrush that allows you to draw in a selected color or pattern, a paint bucket that allows you to "pour" a color or pattern into a section of an image, and a "spray paint" tool that provides an airbrush effect. Other common tools include a "pencil" for adding and deleting individual dots; a "teardrop" for softening edges; and a "fingerpaint" tool that allows you to smudge colors.

One of the most intriguing painting tools found in many image-editing programs is the "Cloning" function. As it is often implemented, you select the tool and click the mouse button after moving the cursor to one portion of an image. When you paint in another part of the image, the portion under which you originally clicked is reproduced as you paint.

Many programs allow you to modify the way these tools work. You can change the size and shape of the brushes, make the tool's effects transparent to one degree or another, or soften the tool's "edge."

Selection Tools

Most image-editing programs also include sophisticated tools that allow you to select a portion of an image for modification. These typically include a marquee tool for selecting rectangular areas and a lasso tool for objects with irregular shapes. Some programs include a "Magic Wand" tool (Figure 4-5) that allows you to click inside an irregular-shaped object to select it automatically. To work properly, there must be a high degree of contrast between the object and the surrounding area.

Once an area of the image is selected, you can move it, duplicate it, or cut-and-paste it to another area or to a different image file. Some programs allow you to stretch or rotate selected image portions. You can also limit certain software operations to the portion of the image inside or outside the selected area, an operation known as masking.

Filters

Most image-editing programs also offer a wide range of image processing features. Basic image-processing func-

Figure 4-5. The "Magic Wand" feature allows you to select an irregular-shaped object.

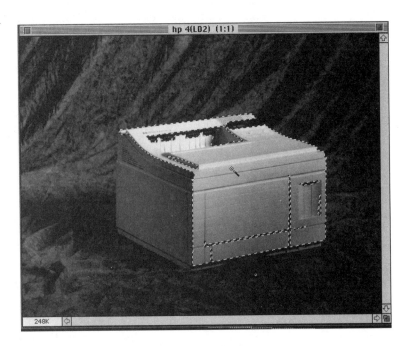

ENHANCING PHOTO CD IMAGES

tions include brightness and contrast control, but many programs go far beyond these. Sharpening "filters," for example, can automatically sharpen the detail in an image. "Blur" filters can produce a softening effect. "Mosaic" filters convert a portion of an image into large-sized pixels (like what you see on television news shows when they are interviewing someone who doesn't want their face seen).

Color Correction

Finally, many image-editing programs offer powerful color correction and calibration features. These features can automatically modify an image to get the best possible output quality on specific models of imagesetters, color printers, or other output devices.

One way that color correction features are implemented is through a function known as a "gamma curve" or "transfer function" editor. This is a linear graph that shows how pixel values in the original image (horizontal axis) correspond to values in the displayed image (vertical axis).

In a normal black-and-white (gray-scale) image, the line runs diagonally from the lower left to upper right, showing a one-to-one correspondence between the two versions of the image. Pixels that were black in the original image are displayed as black, while pixels that were white are represented as white. But if you reverse the line, going from upper left to lower right, the pixels also become reversed. Black pixels in the original image display as white, and white pixels are displayed as black. The result is a negative.

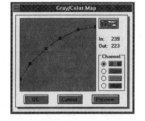

Figure 4-6. A transfer function relates input pixel values from the original image data to transformed pixel values in the displayed image.

By altering the shape and slope of the curve, you can create interesting effects in an image. Increasing the slope, for example, raises the level of contrast by forcing most of the pixels toward the light and dark ends of the spectrum. Raising or lowering the line adjusts brightness. If you reverse the curve for a selected range of tonal values, you can get an effect called solarization in which certain areas appear as negative images and others as positives. By limiting the number of tonal values, you can get an effect called posterization in which the image appears more like a line drawing than a photo.

In a gray-scale image, the relationship between the original photograph and the displayed version can be defined by a single gamma curve. However, in a color image, the relationship is defined by a separate curve for each primary component. Thus, in an RGB image, the image-editing program will allow you to modify the transfer function separately for the red, green, and blue elements.

By modifying the gamma curve, you can adjust an image so that it will print correctly on nearly any output device. For example, if a certain imagesetter tends to darken an image, you can account for this by lightening the image with the gamma curve editor. The problem is knowing just how to modify the transfer curve for the peripheral devices in your system. Programs with automated calibration or color correction features include pre-defined gamma curves designed to modify images for output on a specific printers or imagesetters.

Some of the leading image-editing packages for the Macintosh and PC are profiled below.

Adobe Photoshop

Adobe Photoshop is considered by many designers to be the leading image-editing program for the Macintosh (Figure 4-7). Adobe has also released a Microsoft Windows version that is identical in most respects to the Macintosh version.

Photoshop is a sophisticated program that offers a wide array of features for manipulating photographic images in color or gray-scale. In addition to the standard painting and selection tools found in most image-editing programs, Photoshop supports the use of "plug-ins," small software modules that perform customized image processing, scanning, or other functions. These plug-ins include image

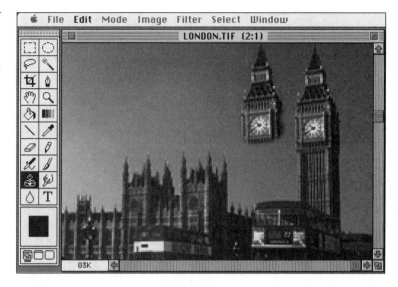

Figure 4-7. Adobe Photoshop features a "clone" tool that can replicate a portion of an image.

filters that can sharpen or soften an image or produce one of many special effects. Others perform image compression or resizing operations. A standard set of plug-ins is included with Photoshop, but many third-party vendors offer their own plug-ins. Because Photoshop is so popular, some developers of competing graphics programs have added the ability to work with Photoshop plug-ins.

One unique aspect of Photoshop is its use of channels that let you isolate certain color elements in an image. In a CYMK image, for example, you can view and modify the cyan, yellow, magenta, and black elements separately. Likewise, in an RGB image, you can view the red, green, and blue elements separately. Photoshop, by the way, makes it easy to convert images among RGB, CYMK, and HSL (hue, saturation, and lightness) color models.

Photoshop also includes extensive functions for separating and printing color images. For example, you can apply color trapping, which causes neighboring colors to slightly overlap, or perform undercolor removal functions, which changes the balance of cyan, yellow, magenta, and black in an image to ensure better quality when the image is printed.

The program uses virtual memory, meaning it can employ the hard disk as an extension of RAM. As a result, you can work with practically any image on a Macintosh with only 2 megabytes of memory. However, virtual disk access is slow, and many image operations require large amounts of memory. For this reason, most serious Photoshop users equip their computers with large amounts of RAM, sometimes as much as 128 megabytes. Even with this kind of memory, some operations involving large, high-resolution images can take hours to complete. Several vendors, including RasterOps, Radius, SuperMac, and Newer Technologies offer accelerator boards specifically aimed at speeding up Photoshop operations.

Fractal Design ColorStudio

Fractal's ColorStudio, which was originally marketed by Letraset, is similar to Photoshop in many ways. The Macintosh-based program supports full 24-bit color and offers a wide array of image processing and manipulation features. It has especially powerful features for creating masks.

One unique feature in ColorStudio is Shapes, a program module that offers drawing tools similar to those found in Adobe Illustrator and Aldus Freehand. Users can create vector-based text or illustrations in Shapes, then have them incorporated into ColorStudio images.

Another useful aspect of ColorStudio is its ability to work with Photoshop plug-ins. This means that third-party image processing products created for Photoshop will also work with ColorStudio. The package itself comes with a wide range of image filters that allow users to apply special effects to an image.

Aldus PhotoStyler

PhotoStyler was developed by a Taiwanese company called U-Lead Systems and is sold by Aldus Corp. (Figure 4-8). It runs under Windows and provides many of the same

Figure 4-8. Aldus PhotoStyler runs under Microsoft Windows.

functions found in Photoshop and ColorStudio. It works with 24-bit color, 8-bit gray-scale, and 1-bit black-and-white images. In addition to working with Photo CD images, PhotoStyler can capture images directly from video frame-grabbers or desktop scanners made by Hewlett-Packard, Microtek, Nikon, and others.

PhotoStyler features an open architecture that allows developers to create plug-in modules. Built into the program are color-correction tools for adjusting brightness, contrast, hue, and saturation. Image filters include two- and three-dimensional, embossing, and mosaic effects. It uses twin clipboards to enhance cut-and-paste operations and also offers powerful masking functions.

PhotoStyler has four palettes that offer a rich set of color options, as well as selection, retouching, and painting tools for altering or adding to an image, repairing scratches and blemishes, and performing cloning and colorization techniques. The palettes "float" on-screen, so the user can move them around to obtain the most efficient arrangement of the display area. A scratch-pad area is available for testing color mixes.

Images can be printed from any PostScript- and Windows-compatible printer or imagesetter. Output options include the ability to specify halftone angle and dot shape, screen frequency and angle, and gray-component replacement and under-color removal when printing color separations.

U-Lead, the company that developed PhotoStyler, offers its own program called ImagePals that provides basic image-enhancement functions. An Album feature allows you to organize and retrieve images, and Enhancer functions allow you to paint, color-correct, apply filters, create special effects, stitch, resize, resample, rotate, and more. Images can also be compressed and decompressed using the JPEG standard.

Micrografx Picture Publisher

Picture Publisher, originally developed by a company called Astral Development, was one of the first image-editing programs to run on the PC. In 1991, Astral Development was acquired by Micrografx Corp., which now sells the Windows-based program as Micrografx Picture Publisher.

This is a full-featured program that can hold its own with an image-editing package on the market. One of its strengths is its extensive calibration features, which automatically modify images for output on specific printers and imagesetters. In addition, it offers a wide array of painting, selection, and image manipulation tools. A Stitch tool allows users to connect two smaller images into one large image with the ability to blend seams.

Picture Publisher can read Photo CD format images directly from a CD-ROM drive. In addition, the program offers JPEG image compression and decompression. It was one of the first programs to support TWAIN, a computer industry standard for communicating with scanners and video digitizers.

ZSoft PhotoFinish

ZSoft's PhotoFinish is an inexpensive image-editing program for Microsoft Windows that has many features found in costlier packages (Figure 4-9). It offers an extensive array of painting, selection, retouching, and image processing tools, and also provides automated calibration functions.

One unique aspect of PhotoFinish is that it provides some features as tools that are normally implemented as filters. For example, a brightness tool allows you to increase or decrease the brightness of areas over which you paint. Sharpen and contrast tools work in a similar manner. Image filters for brightness, contrast, sharpening, and many other operations are available if you want to work on the entire image or a selected portion.

The program also includes a unique "Local Undo" tool that is helpful in creating composite images. The function works like a paintbrush tool, except it undoes the previous operation in the area where you paint. For example, you can paste one image on top of another, then selectively paint out portions of the pasted image.

Figure 4-9. ZSoft's PhotoFinish is a low-cost image-editing program for Microsoft Windows.

A version of PhotoFinish known as "Corel PhotoPaint" is included in CorelDraw, one of the most popular graphics packages for Windows. CorelDraw is primarily a vector-based illustration program, but it can incorporate photographic images. PhotoPaint is one of several modules sold with the package. Others include a business charting program (CorelChart), a presentation program (CorelShow), and an image retrieval program (Mosaic).

Halo Desktop Imager

Media Cybernetics' Halo Desktop Imager, another Windows program, includes a comprehensive set of utilities for facilitating the most frequently encountered tasks in desktop imaging, such as file format conversion, image retouching, and output. It doesn't have the wide range of painting tools found in some of its competitors, but does provide many image enhancement operations. It can directly import Photo CD images (Figure 4-10).

User can enhance less-than-perfect photographs with sharpen, soften, despeckle, and other special effects tools. Other features allow correction of image tonality, contrast,

Figure 4-10. Halo Desktop Imager can directly import Photo CD images.

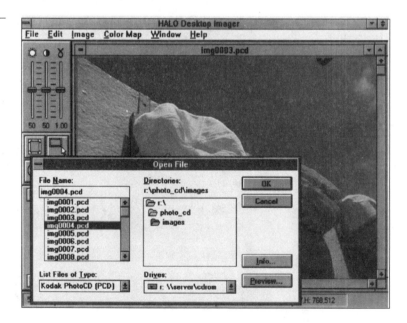

and color balance. In addition to color and gamma correction, you can scale, flip, flop, crop, and rotate images. A "Copy As" function allows you to convert an image to a halftone and copy it to the Clipboard in a single operation. This reduces the time it takes to add multiple images to documents created in other applications.

The software also offers extensive printing (but not color separation) functions. It provides control of halftone, dot-size, angle, lines per inch, and dots per inch, and offers the ability to produce wall-sized posters. By creating printer "test strips," the Halo Desktop Imager allows the user to preview the effects of selected enhancements before final images are printed or exported. With the test strips, the user can decide which brightness, contrast, or gamma settings achieve the desired results based on actual output rather than on the computer monitor.

The Halo Desktop Imager also uses Media Cybernetics' proprietary M/Color technology to present high-quality color images on any 8-, 16- or 24-bit display adapter under Windows. M/Color lets the user mix 24-bit true color, 8-bit palettized, gray-scale, and binary images on the same screen without limit. M/Color also allows the user to adjust and retouch any single image on the screen without affecting the other images.

Image-In Color and Professional

Image-In is a series of modular programs for Microsoft Windows users intended for use with scanners and other image-capture devices. The modules cover such functions as scanning, text-recognition, and image storage and retrieval. However, the company (also called Image-In) offers Image-In Color and Image-In Color Professional for color editing functions. Image-In Color (Figure 4-11) is an inexpensive program that offers basic image enhancement functions. Image-In Color Professional offers a more extensive image-editing functions approaching those found in PhotoStyler and Picture Publisher.

Figure 4-11. Image-In offers a series of modular graphics programs.

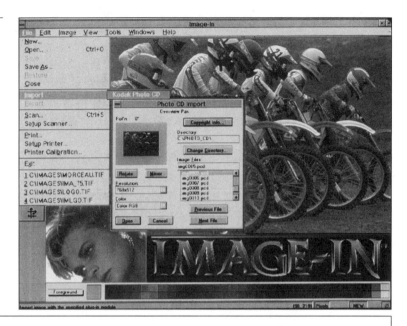

Corporate Image Libraries

APPLICATION BRIEF

Many companies accumulate large files of photographs and illustrations that are stored in filing cabinets. Companies are getting rid of these filing cabinets by storing photo files on Photo CD discs. Using Photo CD offers several advantages. The images on the discs can be copied over and over without the usual losses encountered when copying slides. Storage space requirements are reduced, and inexpensive backup discs can kept at other locations. Finally, and most importantly, image retrieval can be completely automated using the Kodak Image Library system.

The Photo CD Image Library can store up to 10,000 images in a single jukebox that holds 100 discs. Several jukeboxes can be linked to form a larger library. Any image can retrieved in seconds using a computer. Company employees in any location worldwide can access the corporate image library via the company's computer network or electronic mail system. The digital images can be copied directly to computers or output to film or paper.

Software For Color Control

In addition to programs for modifying images, several developers—including Kodak—offer color management systems that automatically adjust images to account for the ways that different scanners, monitors, and output devices handle color (see Chapter Three). The core of these systems are "device profiles" that store information about the color reproduction characteristics of different peripheral devices. As an image passes through the publishing system to final output, the color management software ensures that each device will handle it in a consistent and accurate manner. The aim is to make the color you see the color you get (CYSISYG or sissy-sig) no matter what kind of hardware or software is being used to capture, display, or print the image.

Another approach to color control is a Macintosh program from Electronics for Imaging (EFI) called Cachet. Cachet automates the process of correcting colors by presenting the user with a reference image alongside the working image. The user adjusts the reference image to match a printed version, and the working image is automatically modified to match those color characteristics. A MultiChoice feature lets the user choose the best-looking image from a series of modified versions. The program also includes device profiles for popular printers.

EFI contends that even though Photo CD includes automatic color correction features, the program is still useful with Photo CD images. Photo CD's color correction takes into account the entire frame of the picture. With Cachet, users can apply color correction to a selected portion of an image, which in some cases may result in a noticeable improvement in quality.

Image Enhancement Workstations

An entirely new generation of lower-priced workstations that lend themselves to image processing have become available. These workstations, based on RISC technology, offer more processing power than PCs. All of the major workstation vendors—Digital Equipment, IBM, Hewlett-Packard, Silicon Graphics, NeXT, and Sun Microsystems—are trying to capture the high-end of the imaging and publishing market for computers (Figure 4-12).

Figure 4-12. NeXT Computer is targeting graphic imaging applications for its workstations.

The drawback of workstations is the relatively small selection of imaging and publishing software packages that run under the UNIX operating system used on these machines. However, companies like Island Graphics are developing software packages (Island Write, Draw, Paint) for workstations. Also, Sun and some other computers, even though they operate in a UNIX environment, can run PC and Mac software applications in Windows.

For profesional retouchers of digital images, a complete image enhancement system on a powerful workstations may be what is needed to speed up processing and output

Figure 4-13. Intergraph's image editing workstation consists of a number of components.

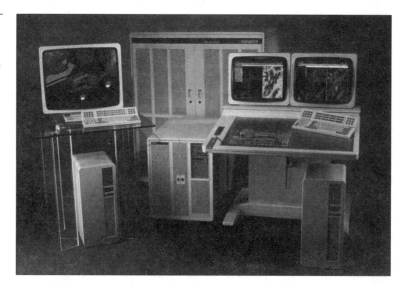

(Figure 4-13). These systems can include very sophisticated enhancement functions and most can already use Photo CDs as their input source.

Complete image enhancement systems are available from Agfa, Barco, Dicomed, EPS, ImageMax, Imapro, Intergraph, Kodak, Management Graphics, Networked Picture Systems, and Superset. There are significant differences in price, functions, and productivity among these and other enhancement systems.

CHAPTER 5

Publishing With Photo CD

The biggest advantage of working with Photo CD instead of slides, transparencies, or prints is that Photo CD images can be brought directly into the computer, where they can be sized, cropped, and enhanced before they are placed in a page layout. Photo CD expands opportunities for the use of color images in electronically produced publications, from simple documents printed on the desktop to commercial newspapers, magazines, and advertisements.

For most publishing applications, the Photo CD Master disc provides good-quality images and is a convenient and reliable storage medium. For high-end publishing applications, the Pro Photo Master CD disc can handle images with resolution approaching what the best prepress rotary scanners can produce. Almost all page layout software packages can handle Photo CD images, either directly or through standard file formats available from Kodak Access software or image enhancement programs.

Besides using Photo CD to store digital images, the Photo CD discs themselves can be used as a publication medium. Portfolio Photo CD discs can hold up to 800 TV-resolution images and Catalog Photo CD discs can store more than 6000 images, which is more than most paper catalogs. These easily prepared Photo CD formats are a convenient way to publish and distribute catalogs, illustrated guides and directories, and yearbooks.

Business-To-Business Product Directories

APPLICATION BRIEF

Catalogs and directories listing commercial and industrial products and services can reach a size of several thousand pages, making them cumbersome to use. Computer databases speed the search for information, but do not supply pictures. Photo CD Catalog discs offer a way to bring product pictures and printed descriptions together in a form that can be easily searched and retrieved.

Catalog Photo CD discs with several thousand color photos and text can be interactively searched by customers using a computer. The disc can contain phone numbers for fast ordering.

In the sporting goods market, to show their whole sports equipment line more easily, one manufacturer has developed a series of Photo CD discs for use in presentations to sporting goods stores, team owners, and managers.

Sporting goods promotion image from a Photo CD Catalog disc.

Photo CD Catalog

With the Kodak Photo CD Catalog disc, people can interactively view and listen to catalogs on their television sets or computers. The Kodak Photo CD Catalog format allows easy production of on-disc catalogs containing thousands of pictures: vacation destinations, works of art, retail products, and so on. The pictures can be formatted into catalog pages on the screen, complete with text, graphics, a table of contents, and chapters—even voice and music.

People who play the discs in home Photo CD players connected to their TV can see on-screen menus that will lead them through the catalog at the touch of a remote control. Computer users can run Kodak Browser software to locate images with simple keyword searches.

With the Kodak Photo CD Catalog format, more than 6000 video-resolution images can be stored for display on TV and computer monitors. More images can be stored in thumbnail form. The Catalog format uses only the lower-resolution Base images, so they cannot be used to make photo-quality prints. However, their quality is ideal for video display. For viewing Photo CD Catalog images on a TV set, a Photo CD player or CD-I player is needed. To bring the catalog onto a computer screen, the computer must have a Photo CD-compatible CD-ROM XA drive.

Using a Kodak Photo CD Catalog disc in a home Photo CD player is easy. After the disc has been inserted into the player, a menu screen greets the viewer and offers several branches that can be followed. On a clothing catalog disc, there might be Men's, Women's, and Children's sections. From there, additional menus help guide the viewer to Men's Sweaters or Children's Shoes.

All the normal Photo CD player functions are available with a Kodak Photo CD Catalog disc, including zoom and pan. Sound, if any, is played as each image appears on the screen.

Each picture on the disc has a unique number that can be revealed by panning to the right side of the image. This feature can also be used as an order number or a key to the order number.

Running a Kodak Photo CD Catalog disc on a desktop computer gives the viewer even more options. Like the person viewing catalog images on a home TV set, the computer user can zoom, pan, and listen to sound associated with each image. In addition to searching for images through on-screen menus, the user can take advantage of the Kodak Browser software resident on the catalog disc to conduct keyword searches.

For example, the keywords Men, Sweaters, and Blue might automatically display all of the images with blue men's sweaters. Searches of this type are faster than searching through page after page for the right item. This feature could help make image library or museum catalog searches dramatically more efficient.

Organizations that want to create their own catalog on a Photo CD Catalog disc need a graphics-capable desktop computer and Kodak Photo CD Catalog authoring software. With the help of the software, they will be able to select images from their existing Kodak Photo CD Master discs, then add graphics, text, and sound to create a program script. This script is used by the Photo CD system to make the finished discs.

Small quantities of finished Kodak Photo CD Catalog discs can be produced by a photofinisher or on a user's own compact disc writer. Compact disc mastering houses can economically produce the larger quantities of discs needed for mass distribution.

For large catalogs, images can be stored in the Kodak Image Library system and automatically retrieved when catalog discs are made. Also, the low-resolution images on catalog discs can be linked to the Image Library to allow access to high-resolution 4Base and 16Base images.

Photo CD Portfolio

Kodak Photo CD Portfolio discs combine sound, text, graphics, and interactive branching with photographs, and open up many new consumer and commerical applications for Photo CD.

Portfolio discs can hold up to 800 images at TV-resolution or one hour of audio CD-quality stereo sound or any combination of images and sound, such as 400 images and 30 minutes of sound. The Portfolio discs are created from either Photo CD Master discs or other Photo CD Portfolio discs, and not directly from 35mm slides or other film-based images.

Both Photo CD Master and Photo CD Portfolio discs have a feature known as "calls branching." This means the discs can display images in different sequences as determined by interaction from the user.

Like the Photo CD Master format, the Photo CD Portfolio format lets users add sound, text, and graphics to their pictures. For example, they may create audio captions to accompany the pictures on a family tree or for a multimedia-style business presentation.

Most applications for Kodak Photo CD Portfolio discs will probably be found in one of three categories: personal pictures, business presentations, and pre-mastered pre-recorded discs for sale through retail channels.

Personal Pictures

Personal applications for portfolio discs include family albums, where the viewer can look at pictures of grandparents, birthday celebrations, or even the family dog, just by choosing the appropriate branch from an on-screen menu. As the pictures are displayed on either a Photo CD player or a computer's CD-ROM drive, sound or graphics linked to the image will also play. A photo of grandparents, for example, might include on-screen text noting the year and location, along with reminiscences of the period in grandma's voice.

To create Kodak Photo CD Portfolio discs, customers must use special authoring software at Photo CD service bureaus and photofinishers. The customer brings in their Kodak Photo CD Master or Portfolio discs and audio tapes or CDs, and uses the authoring software to assemble the material on the Portfolio disc.

Easy-to-use templates will speed assembly of the most popular applications, such as family trees, weddings, and birthdays. Once the consumer has assembled the program, it is turned over to the photofinisher, who creates the Portfolio disc on the Photo CD Imaging Workstation (PIW).

Business Presentations

Businesses can produce their own Photo CD discs for presentations and distribution. In addition to business presentations, this application area includes new product introductions, real estate listings, travelogs, and other promotional materials.

The key difference between the business and the personal picture categories is in how the discs are created. Business users with properly configured desktop computers and Kodak's authoring software can create their own Portfolio discs and produce them with the Kodak Photo CD 200 Writer.

Pre-mastered Discs

As the use of Photo CD increases and Photo CD playing devices become widely installed, it is expected that the Photo CD Portfolio disc will become a standard format for multimedia titles that are mass produced under a brand name.

Some companies are planning to use the Portfolio discs to publish guided tours of major museums with narrated summaries of fine art collections (complete with mood-setting music). Another company is planning to publish a series of children's books on Portfolio discs.

Production of pre-mastered discs begins at a desktop computer or workstation. However, final production of large quantities of discs would take place at a compact disc mastering house, similar to those that stamp audio CDs.

Conventional Publishing and Photo CDs

The same digital revolution that spawned Photo CD has also had a dramatic effect on the way pages are prepared for printing. What began as "desktop publishing"—a way to produce black-and-white pages on inexpensive laser printers—has evolved into a wide ranging application that has intruded into the furthest reaches of print production. Programs like QuarkXPress and Aldus PageMaker make it possible to produce almost any kind of publication using a Macintosh or PC-compatible computer.

Instead of going to traditional color houses, many publishers are turning to service bureaus equipped with PostScript imagesetters to produce color separations from files prepared on a Macintosh or PC. It is even possible to send color pages directly from a computer system to a printing press.

Photo CDs will dramatically alter the way photographs are used for publishing. Desktop scanners have long been key components in computer publishing systems because of their ability to scan photographs and other images for use in electronic page layouts. With Photo CD, computer users now have an excellent alternative for quality image-capture.

While there will still be a need for scanners, Photo CD offers many advantages over image scanning. Scanner users must often color-correct their images after they have been scanned. Images on a Photo CD disc are color-corrected before they are recorded. Scanned images must be stored on a hard drive or similar storage device.

Photo CD images come stored on a convenient medium: the Photo CD disc itself. Though there are plenty of scanners capable of producing images of high quality, many scanners, especially flatbed and hand-held models, do not measure up. With Photo CD images, users are assured of a uniform level of quality.

One of the real conveniences of Photo CD is that users can import a version of an image close to the desired resolution without opening an entire Image Pac of five images. Images can be imported in TIFF or any other format by using Kodak Access software or software that has been developed for individual programs.

Another advantage of Photo CD is its use of low-resolution thumbnail images. Some desktop publishing packages offer a feature called automatic picture replacement (APR) that is especially useful when working with large color images (Figure 5-1).

Figure 5-1. The picture replacement function in Aldus PageMaker is a useful tool for Photo CD users.

You can import a low-resolution version of the image to position, crop, and scale in your page layout. Because the image consumes less file space than the high-resolution version, it is easier to work with. When the file is printed, the software automatically replaces the low-resolution image with the high-resolution version.

The New Newspaper Morgue

APPLICATION BRIEF

A newspaper morgue is where published stories are kept in reference files, along with other reference material. Journalists still use the macabre term—which grew out of the expression that published stories were "dead"—to refer to the newspaper reference library, which now is likely to be a computer database. Photographs and illustrations are increasingly being stored on CD-ROM discs, and many newspapers are choosing Photo CD because of its image quality and compatiblity with a wide range of publishing software.

With the advent of high-quality visual images on the Photo CD, newspapers can now library their photo images in a form that can be brought into the system quickly by any editor sitting at his desk. With a CD-ROM player in a workstation, high-quality photo images will be available on screen rather than bringing them photographs from the library or the storage room.

Some newspapers offer their photos as a service to outside buyers. Photo Catalog CDs or Portfolio CDs offer an easy way of providing reproductions in digital form.

Magazine and book publishers also are planning to store published images on Photo CD discs. The use of Photo CD as a standard for image storage opens up the way for wider distribution of digital images.

Applied Graphics Technologies (AGT) is working with its clients in the magazine, commercial publishing, and advertising markets to create a large news and illustrative image collection that will be maintained by AGT. The photos and illustrations are being scanned and put on Photo CD discs by AGT, and Kodak has agreed to market the images through the Kodak Picture Exchange service.

Standards in Prepress

One thorny issue for electronic publishing users is the absence of standards. The high-end prepress systems used by traditional color separation houses are proprietary. That is, all components come from a single manufacturer, and cannot be "mixed or matched" with components from other manufacturers. In contrast, microcomputer-based systems are open, meaning that an installation can include scanners, monitors, computers, and output devices from different vendors.

The problem with open systems is making sure each component knows how to talk to the others. It is more than a matter of going from disc to display to output. At each stage of the process, each component adds its own "accent" to the way the image is reproduced. Accounting for these variations is one of the functions of the color management systems described earlier in Chapter Three.

It would be ideal if the colors in a photograph or screen image could be exactly matched by the final image on a printed page. Color management software is bringing this closer, but there are limits to what color control can achieve.

The problem boils down to the range of colors that can be produced on press. The dynamic color range that the human eye can see (using simple whole numbers) is 0 through 10. Using the same scale, what film can see is possibly 2 through 8. The printed page can produce a range of 3 through 6 (Figure 5-2). In technical terms, the range of colors that can be reproduced by a particular device is known as its color "gamut."

The core of a color management system is a "color space." A color space is a model for how colors can be described. An RGB color space, for example, can be seen as a triangle in

Figure 5-2. The printed page has a lesser dynamic range than what the eye can see.

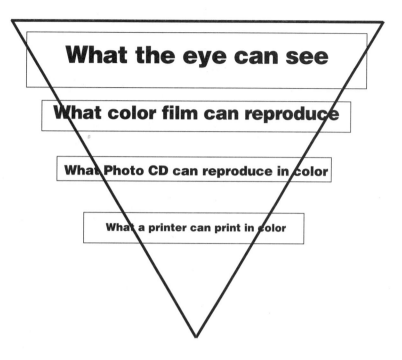

which each of the vertices represents red, green, or blue. Any color that can be displayed on a RGB monitor can be defined as a point—a certain combination of red, green, and blue—within the triangle (this is actually an oversimplification, but serves to illustrate the point).

Color management systems use a pre-defined color space as a consistent reference point for how color is perceived. Colors in the original image are translated into the equivalent values in the reference color space, ensuring that they will be handled consistently no matter what device is used to display or print them. Most color spaces are based on a set of international standards known as CIE. Kodak has developed a color space called PhotoYCC for the Photo CD system in order to maintain consistent values for colors.

When Photo CD images are encoded, Kodak's color management software modifies them to match certain CIE standards. They are stored as if they were scanned on a certain scanner (known technically as the "reference image-capture device") at a certain level of illumination (known as "CIE Standard Illuminant D65"). The characteristics of the reference image-capturing device are defined in part by CCIR 709, an international recommendation for high-definition television production and exchange.

RGB image signals are converted to PhotoYCC values in three steps. First, a "nonlinear transformation" is applied. This means that the image is translated according to a transfer curve that modifies the values of each pixel. This nonlinearity allows rapid, efficient conversion of the RGB signals to a format in which they can be displayed without sacrificing gamut, color fidelity, or device-independent performance.

Next, the resulting values are converted to one luma (light) and two chroma (color) components that define their position in the color space. Finally, these three components are converted to 8-bit data for storage. The RGB values delivered by the reference image-capturing device are not constrained to positive values. The PhotoYCC scheme expands the color gamut (the range of colors that can be described) to include colors outside the limits defined by CCIR 709 for computer displays.

With PhotoYCC, the color-encoding scheme is not limited by any display device. But for publishing systems, PhotoYCC has some problems. The question is whether existing color separation systems will easily interpret the PhotoYCC values. The real issue may be the number of different systems that Photo CD can be plugged into with the least amount of problems.

To some people, PhotoYCC represents an improvement over the previous CIE model. But we are still limited by the printing process. The eye can see a broad range of colors. The range of colors that can be shown on film is not quite as broad, but still good. However, the range of colors that can be produced on press is less than half of what the eye can see. This may disturb a purist, but in the real world the ultimate question is whether it is good enough.

Today's color photographic materials are superb. Our printing capabilities are good, both in black-and-white and in color, but a printed piece does not match a photographic print or a transparency. The image produced by the Photo CD is a photorealistic image of high quality that will meet printing in the digital age.

Software For Publishing

Once the sole province of lead type and metal engravings, printing has moved universally to the desktop computer. Today, magazines like *Time* and *Newsweek*, as well as major newspapers, meet tighter deadlines than ever before using desktop publishing software. What was once the province of the highly skilled page make-up artist has moved to the desktop, sometimes with outstanding results, at other times disastrously.

The first impact of desktop publishing came with the introduction of the Macintosh computer. For many publishing organizations, the Macintosh has become a *de facto* standard. However, some prefer to use PCs because of their lower cost. Other platforms, such as the IBM PS/2, Sun and Silicon Graphics workstations, and the NeXT computer also can be part of the production loop.

What makes desktop publishing possible is the software that has been developed to drive computers and peripherals. A number of excellent software programs exist for desktop publishing. Some of the leading packages are described below.

Aldus PageMaker

Though PageMaker was not the very first desktop publishing program, it is widely credited with being one of the key products that ushered in the application. In fact, it was Aldus Corp. president Paul Brainerd who coined the term "desktop publishing." Today, PageMaker is available in versions for the Macintosh and Microsoft Windows.

PageMaker uses what is known as a "pasteboard" metaphor for page design (Figure 5-3). Users are presented with an electronic version of a layout board on which they can place text or graphics. Text can be imported from most of the popular word processing programs, and graphics can be imported in a wide range of vector- and raster-based formats. In both cases, files are imported by means of a Place command in the File menu. Users can also produce text using a built-in Story Editor, and can add simple graphic elements such as boxes and rules from a built-in toolbox.

When a graphic file is placed in PageMaker, the user can crop it using a cropping tool or scale it by dragging handles

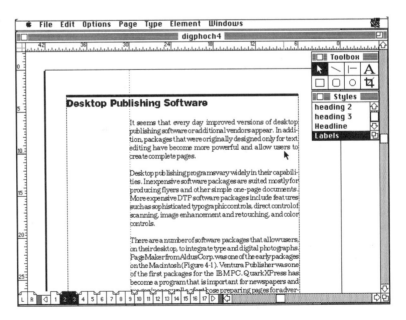

Figure 5-3. Aldus PageMaker is one of the most popular desktop publishing programs on the market today.

that appear when the image is selected. When a gray-scale TIFF or PICT image is placed, the user can modify certain image settings using the Image Control dialog box. However, the Image Control settings do not affect color images.

PageMaker includes the built-in ability to produce color separations directly from the Print dialog box. You can also print a composite image on a color PostScript printer. However, if you want to print separations that include color TIFF files—presumably the format in which Photo CD images will be placed—you need to use a utility program called Aldus PrePrint.

To produce separations, you first use PageMaker to print the file to disk in a special format known as OPI (for Open Prepress Interface). You then open the OPI file in PrePrint and use menu selections to produce the separations. One advantage of the OPI format is that it allows you to use a low-resolution version of an image for placement purposes. When you use PrePrint to produce the separations, you can link the publication to a high-resolution version of the image.

QuarkXPress

QuarkXPress, with its sophisticated typographic and color publishing tools, is a favorite among graphic artists, advertising agencies, package designers, and magazine publishers. First developed for the Macintosh, it is also available in a version for Microsoft Windows.

Graphics in Quark are placed by means of a Picture frame positioned in the page layout. The user first draws the frame, then chooses a menu option to import the graphic. The size of the frame determines how the picture is cropped: it's as if the frame were a window through which you can see the imported image. The picture can be resized by dragging on handles that appear around the picture block or by entering reduction or enlargement values in a dialog box.

Figure 5-4.
QuarkXPress is a
favorite among design
professionals.

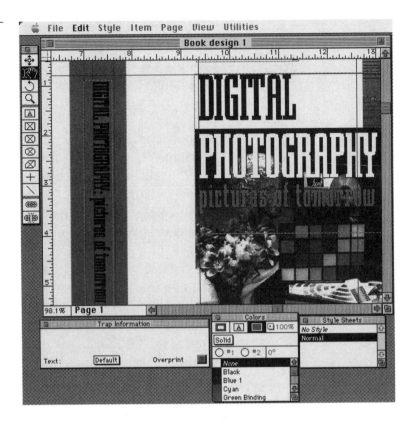

Like PageMaker, QuarkXPress includes functions that
allow you to make modifications to imported images.
Unlike PageMaker, these functions work with color images
as well as gray-scale. When an image is selected, the Quark
Style menu that normally offers text styling commands
instead offers a series of options for modifying the image.
You can apply different levels of contrast using predefined
settings or an "Other Contrast" option that calls up a
gamma curve editor (see Chapter Four). You can also
choose the halftone line screen and screen angle for the
printed image.

To produce color separations that include color TIFF images, you need to use a third-party QuarkXTension.
QuarkXTensions are utility programs that work with
QuarkXPress. Several vendors offer XTensions that allow
output of color separations from QuarkXPress files. Elec-

tronics for Imaging, developer of Cachet and the EfiColor Color Management System, offers a QuarkXTension that incorporates many of the color matching features in those programs. The product includes device profiles for monitors, printers, and offset presses that ensure consistent handling of color images.

Ventura Publisher

Ventura Publisher, an early leader in the PC desktop publishing market, is available in versions for MS-DOS, Windows, and the Macintosh. Unlike PageMaker or QuarkXPress, which offer a highly interactive approach to page design, Ventura uses more of a batch-oriented approach.

Text created in a word processor is flowed into a publication and formatted according to a style sheet set up by the user. These style sheets consist of "tags" that define the look of various page elements, such as headlines, subheads, or body text. Users can apply tags by means of codes entered in the word processor or by highlighting text that has been flowed into a Ventura document. Though Quark and PageMaker both include style sheet options, Ventura places much greater emphasis on its use of style sheets. The ability of style sheets to speed document production—along with automated section numbering and other functions—makes Ventura ideal for production of books, directories, technical manuals, and other structured documents.

Graphics in Ventura are imported into frames that are placed on the page. Images can be scaled and cropped either by dragging on handles that appear at the edge of the frame or by entering values in a dialog box. Supported color file formats include TIFF and PCX.

In an effort to take advantage of the growing interest in desktop color, Ventura Software has introduced a series of auxiliary products that enhances the program's ability to work with color images. They are available in Windows versions only.

Two of these programs, Ventura Scan and Ventura Separator, are included when you buy the basic Ventura Publisher for Windows package. Ventura Scan is a program that allows the user to control a scanner from within Ventura Publisher. Ventura Separator allows production of color separations, also from within Ventura. It includes controls that allow you to modify the brightness, contrast, color saturation, and sharpness of the image. It also provides control over halftone screening angles and frequency,

Catalogs on Disc

APPLICATION BRIEF

Home shoppers can use their own television sets to browse through electronic catalogs on Photo CD Catalog discs. Over 6000 color product pictures can be stored on a single disc, along prices, product description, and ordering information. Home viewers can browse through various categories of products or jump directly to a specific product. The color choices for a product can be shown on the screen.

L. L. Bean, one of the leading catalog clothing retailers in the U.S. is interested in trying out Photo CD Catalogs. Chris McCormick, vice president of the company's advertising and direct marketing, said, "L. L. Bean is proud of its reputation of providing superior customer service, and is constantly looking for new and innovative ways to enhance its leadership position in the catalog industry. The Kodak Photo CD Catalog disc format should provide a new, efficient catalog delivery system to home shoppers around the world. We plan to work with Kodak to fully explore the system's application in customer communications, and other aspects of our operations as well."

and offers sophisticated prepress functions like dot gain correction and undercolor removal.

In addition to Separator, Ventura offers a program called Ventura ColorPro that offers more extensive color separation and correction features. These include an electronic densitometer for measuring color values, gray-component replacement, automatic picture balance, and unsharp masking. In creating the program, the developers attempted to duplicate the kinds of features found in high-end color separation systems.

Ventura also offers PicturePro, a color image-editing program with features similar to those in Adobe Photoshop. One unique aspect of the program is its use of separate painting and drawing "layers." The painting layer is used to modify raster images (such as from Photo CD), while the drawing layer is used to modify object-oriented vector graphics.

Getting the Right Image for Publishing

One question that desktop publishing users must contend with concerns the optimal resolution of images used in a page layout. Ultimately, this is determined by the size and line screen of the image that will be ultimately printed. This, in turn, depends on the kind of press the publication will be printed on, the kind of paper that will be used, and the kind of image quality desired by the publisher.

To play it safe, it might be tempting to use images with the highest possible resolution. However, this is not always wise. As resolution grows, so does the file space consumed by the image. This has implications not only for file storage, but also for the computer system's ability to handle the image. For example, screen redraws on a 300-dpi, 24-bit color images are much slower than redraws for a 150-dpi image unless you have a graphics accelerator. In addition, much of the data in an image file is wasted if the resolution is too high.

If your software supports automatic picture replacement, you can work with a low-resolution version of an image when creating your page layout. When the page is finally printed, the software replaces the low-resolution version with the high-resolution version. However, this solution works only if the image does not have to be modified in a program like Adobe Photoshop.

To determine which of the five Photo CD image resolutions to use, you must know the halftone line screen at which your document will be printed and the final size of the image on your page. In general, the larger the final image size and the finer the line screen, the larger the image file size you must use.

It's important to understand that each halftone dot on the printed page corresponds roughly to one 8-bit pixel; Each color dot can be derived from three 8-bit pixels. Sampling theory says you should use twice as many pixels as halftone dots to compensate for noise in the image. So the number of pixels you need per inch is about twice your halftone line screen.

For example, if your image will be printed with a longer dimension of 5 inches and a 100-line halftone screen, you will need at least 1000 pixels (2x100x5) across in your Photo CD image. Since the Base image only offers 768 pixels (refer to Figure 2-17), you must use the next higher level, 4Base, which offers 1536 pixels in the longer dimension. Figure 5-5 shows the maximum size at which you can print each of the five Photo CD component images. Note that the maximum size decreases as the halftone line screen increases.

The above discussion assumes you are using images from the Photo CD disc at full frame. If you will be cropping the

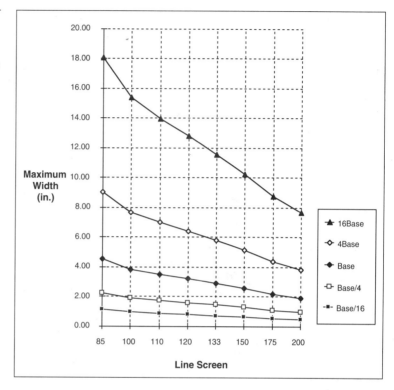

Figure 5-5. The maximum recommended full-frame reproduction size for Photo CD images at various line screens. (Copyright 1993 Micro Publishing Press)

image before printing it, you must adjust your calculations accordingly.

At what resolution should images be scanned? It depends in part on the size of the image when it is printed. If you are going no larger than 4 x 5 with a 4 x 5 original, you can make the scan at 300 dpi and achieve a sampling ratio that will give you a 150 line screen with adequate information. Scanning more than 300 dpi would produce useless information.

The same applies to a 35mm film image. Let's say we want an image four times the size of the original 35mm image. We have to have a resolution that is at least four times whatever the screen value is. So if we use the 150 line screen again as our base and multiply that by four, the resolution we need is 600 dpi. With the Photo CD, we would use the 4 Base image since it has a resolution of 1034 x 1536 or almost twice the 600 x 900 resolution we need.

With a 35mm film scanned to a Photo CD, you would calculate that with a 150 line screen for printing, you could only go to an 8 x 10 inch final image. For a larger final image or a higher line screen resolution, you would ordinarily have to scan the original image on a high-end drum scanner.

However, the Photo CD system used interpolation algorithms to increase the apparent resolution of the scanned image. This technique has been successfully applied with flatbed scanners where resolutions of 600, 800, and even 1200 dpi have been achieved by interpolation. The algorithms calculate intervening values by averaging the pixels on every side of the decompressed pixels.

CHAPTER 6

Legal Implications of Photo CD

From the legal point of view, photographs stored on Photo CDs for home use are no different than any snapshot that a family owns. However, when it comes to commercial use—in advertising, magazines, newspapers, television, and multimedia—the legal aspects of copyright are important to the owner of the image rights and the user of the images.

Digital images, such as the photographs stored on Photo CD discs, present a special legal problem. These images can be easily copied and altered with computers and readily available software. Copying a copyrighted image for commercial use is illegal. But if the image is altered, who owns the altered image? Does the owner of an image have the right to prohibit alterations to it? In some cases, an image may have been altered so much that it bears little or no resemblance to the original.

The basic protection provided by Photo CD is that the actual recording of image—the pattern of pits burned in by the laser—cannot be altered once it is made. The Photo CD disc is a write-once medium. Once a roll of film has been recorded on a Photo CD, the disc can serve as proof of ownership in the same way that the developed film does. Original images on a Photo CD disc can be used as a basis for contesting altered images.

For professional photographers, the copyright and water-mark identifiers developed by Kodak for the Pro Photo CD Master discs can serve as a means of protecting image rights. Both provide unmistakable notification that that the image is copyrighted. In addition, Photo CD allows encryption of images stored, which can prevent unauthorized copying of the images.

Image Ownership and Rights

Photographers have sold rights to their work for more than 100 years. The Copyright Revision Act of 1976 replaced a 1909 statute that did not provide coverage for use of copyrighted material in radio, movies, television, and computers. Before the 1976 revision, the person who hired the photographer was considered to be the copyright owner, unless there was some agreement that the copyright was the property of the photographer. Today, unless there is a written and specific agreement with the client, the photograph, as soon as it is created, is the property of the photographer.

Protection of original work dates back to the time of the writing of the United States Constitution. This protection is extended by the copyright act.

The first form of protection is copyright. To exert the right of authorship, it is important for photographers to identify their work clearly, marking every image produced with the word *Copyright,* or the symbol © or (C), as well as the year of creation or first publication and the name of the owner of the copyright. Many photo stock agencies add a slash and their name to the copyright notice to indicate their involvement in the copyright process.

Under current law, the copyright begins at the time the work is created and continues for the life of the photographer plus 50 years. If the work is made for hire or published using a pseudonym or without a name, the work has a copyright for 75 years from the first publication or 100 years from creation, whichever is the shorter time.

In 1989, the U.S. became a member of the Berne Convention, which does not require a formal indication of copyright on the work. But legal customs do not change overnight, and for safety's sake, it is best if the copyright notice is used. It is like an insurance policy; it gives the copyright holders a stronger case should someone misuse their photographs and images.

Copyright Registration

In the United States, as well as in many other countries, it is possible to register a copyrighted photograph. Registration is handled through the Registrar of Copyrights, Library of Congress, Washington, D.C. 20559, phone (202) 479-0700.

A one-page form is available for registering photographs in Class VA (Visual Arts). The statement includes a description of what was created, the author's age, and information on whether the new work is based on or incorporates something that has already been published.

The filing fee is $20 for each application, and you need to send two nonreturnable samples of the work being registered; 8 x 10-inch size or smaller is preferred. Every photograph must have a caption, which can be a simple title.

It is possible to register many photographs at the same time using a proof sheet of a roll of film. The thumbnail proof sheet from a Photo CD could also be used for bulk registration.

If an unregistered photograph is published, registering it within three months of its publication will protect the work. Many publishers automatically copyright all of their material used in their publications, so professional photographers should take care to preserve their rights by demanding recognition of their copyright ownership. It is important to remember that once a copyright is lost, it can never be regained. The simple act of marking the images will protect your work and prevent its unauthorized use.

Derivative Works

Derivative work based on one or more pre-existing works is covered in the Copyright Act. To encourage innovation, U.S. copyright law allows a degree of liberty in using the work of others as an inspiration for a new work.

When a derivation is registered for copyright, the description must state what the work is based on or whether it incorporates another person's work. The description includes editorial revisions, elaborations, or other modifications.

The problem is that the law did not anticipate the era of the digital photograph and the manipulation opportunities that this technology presents. Images on a Photo CD disc can be copied into a computer. With today's software, it is possible to transform, adapt, and in many ways modify a photograph until the derivative no longer looks at all like the original.

Legally, that original work is the property of the photographer and all rights to it belong to the photographer. That's why it is so important for the photographer or photo stock agency (if one is involved) to specifically state that derivative works are the property of the photographer and a copy of the derivation must be returned to the holder of the copyright.

To the best of our knowledge, no legal cases have yet appeared involving derivative photographs. There have been cases in which musicians have been sued for taking pieces of someone's recorded musical performances and placing it on another CD. This has even occurred with symphonic music. As the music cases progress through the courts, their outcomes may indicate how derivative photographs will be treated when cases arise with them.

Clip-art Photographs

APPLICATION BRIEF

Clip-art photographs on CD discs, sold as complete files of 100 or more images, are becoming popular among desktop publishers as an easy way of adding photographic images to pages. The clip-art photos are also popular with speakers who use them in their presentations. Clip-art photos on Photo CD discs offer additional possibilities to both users and vendors. The ease of use of Photo CD images and their standardized quality will benefit the user. The Photo CD system also offers various image resolutions that can be selected to match the output requirements.

For clip-art vendors, Photo CD offers an inexpensive way to create digitized images on a CD disc. Images on Photo CD Master discs are suitable for mass distribution, while images on Catalog discs offer the vendor the opportunity to send out low-resolution samples of the photographs available. Professional photographers, stock houses, and clip-art vendors can use Pro Photo CD discs for high-quality photographs and encrypt the images, allowing the user only to view the low-resolution version. Upon payment of a royalty, a code to unlock the image can be sent to the user. With image encryption, the use of high-resolution versions of images can be controlled.

Desktop publishing and imaging software packages will also contain clip-art photographs on a Photo CD disc in the future.

Legal Pitfalls

The invasion of privacy becomes even more sensitive when a publication uses a computer to alter a photographic image. A famous instance of such image manipulation was the publication in a major national magazine of the head of Oprah Winfrey on the body of Ann Margaret. Undoubtedly, both of the original photographs had model releases, but they were used inappropriately, thus creating the potential for an invasion of privacy lawsuit.

False light is when a publication falsely attributes a statement or opinion to someone. If a photograph is involved, the photographer can be charged along with the publication.

Under current U.S. law, when a photograph is copied or closely imitated, infringement can be claimed and a lawsuit filed for actual or statutory damages. Statutory damages can range from $500 to $20,000, and can increase to $100,000 if a "willful infringement" can be proved. If the judgment is for "innocent infringement," the award for damages can be as little as $200.

Because they involve federal copyright laws, infringement cases wind up in federal court. Because of the difficulty and cost of of arguing a case in federal court, there is great incentive to settle out of court. If a photographer can establish proper filing of copyright of the infringed photograph, it is more likely that the infringer will settle a case rather than have it go to a trial.

Contracts

Ordinarily, without a contract that is specific, the buyer thinks he or she is getting all rights while the photographer thinks the rights are limited. That is why a written contract is necessary—it specifies what rights are being sold to the buyer.

Marketing Stock Photos on Photo CD

APPLICATION BRIEF

Many of the photos used in advertising, annual reports, magazines, books, and multimedia are supplied by stock photo agencies. In the past, customers would be sent stacks of duplicate transparencies of the subject they need and they would then select the image they wished to purchase. With Photo CD, an entirely new way of handling these images is developing.

Stock photo agencies now can send low-resolution images on Photo CD Catalog discs to prospective customers. Included with the images on the disc are instructions on how to order the high-resolution version of the images. Another method is to send the client a Pro Photo CD disc that has both low-resolution images for viewing and encrypted high-resolution images, which can be unlocked when the client places an order.

Some stock photo agencies are enthusiastic about Photo CDs potential in their market. Craig Aurness is director of Westlight Stock Photo Agency, one of the most recognized and respected names in the stock photography industry. He said, "Westlight has been preparing for the anticipated growth and changes in the industry. We believe that digital technology and multimedia applications will provide an enormous demand for still images, stimulating tremendous growth for our industry.

A stock photo catalog disc. (permission to reproduce courtesy Eastman Kodak Company)

"Westlight is excited about the opportunity to work with Kodak on the expansion and validation of this vision in the areas of image storage, access, and exchange. We intend to publish our image catalog utilizing the Kodak Photo CD Catalog format."

In addition, Westlight Stock Photo Agency is providing images to the Kodak Picture Exchange network.

When buying a digital image on a Photo CD disc, some clients think they will own all the digital data. That is a very good reason for putting a copyright notice in the digital image file and on the Photo CD disc.

If a buyer plans to modify a digital image, the contract should spell out the modification rights. Some kinds of modifications to the image can be prohibited. The contract should also state that all rights not specifically assigned to the buyer are retained by the copyright owner.

Releases—More Than One Kind

Photography, artwork, and many other kinds of graphic services are priced according to how they are used. Rights can be for a one-time use, limited use, or unlimited use, and are priced accordingly.

Most photographers are aware of the fact that a model release is required for photographs taken of a person. If the individual photographed is a minor, then the consent of the parents is required. The responsibility for obtaining the model release lies with the photographer.

The model release still does not totally protect the photographer from the possibility of libel, false light, or invasion of privacy. Consider an example where a photograph for which there is a model release is used in a newspaper or magazine along with a caption or headline that inaccurately describes the situation for which the release was obtained. This could be grounds for libel litigation. If a photograph of the model was made with one intent and is used in another context, the model could file a lawsuit that claims misuse. For example, the photographer might shoot a picture of "a model crying," then sell it to a newspaper that runs it with a caption indicating that the person was in tears after being convicted in a court.

There is another type of release—a property release—that is often overlooked but important if a photograph is going to be used widely. A picture of a home, for example, if used to publicize something, must have a property release from the property owner.

Photo CD Licensing

Whether you make Photo CD discs by recording each one individually or by stamping them on a CD press for mass distribution, you still have to acquire the necessary image rights from copyright owners. However, when mass production is planned, the publisher must also remember that the Photo CD disc contains software and proprietary copyrighted information from Philips and Kodak.

To mass produce Photo CDs by pressing, it is necessary to obtain a license from Philips and Kodak. Photo CD licensing procedure information can be obtained by calling 1-800-242-2424, extension 53.

Clip-Art Photographs

Digital clip art gives desktop publishers a fast, easy, and inexpensive source of drawings, illustrations, and photographs. Until the advent of CD-ROM discs, providing color photographs for computer users was difficult. Now Photo CD makes it possible for clip-art providers to have color photographs digitized and stored on a disc at very low cost. For desktop publishing, clip-art photo discs are a bonanza, offering unlimited use photos for the purchase price.

Professional photographers worry that clip-art photos will destroy part of their market for images, since these photos cost as little as $1 each. Of greater concern to professional photographers is the fear that an unscrupulous clip-art provider will use their copyrighted photographs without seeking permission and without paying royalties or fees. The clip-art provider may try to disguise the copied photograph by altering it slightly.

The usual legal recourse available in these situations is to sue the offending party. Digital images stored on Photo CD discs can help the photographer to prove ownership of the images involved in the lawsuit.

Some companies have been buying the rights to entire collections of work. Microsoft, the developer of Windows and other popular software products, has formed a division to purchase art, photographs, and other original works for use in CD-ROM products.

If large companies buy up the rights to photo collections and begin distributing them on discs and via electronic networks, professional photographers may find that their market for many types of photographs is severely curtailed.

The Legal Outlook

The copyright waters are murky. With the increasing use of computer imaging techniques that allow combination and modification of images, it can be expected that cases of infringement and unauthorized derivatives, as well as libel, invasion of privacy, and other lawsuits, will proliferate.

Copyright Protection

The basic protection for professional photographers is clearly to mark all work with a copyright notice. If a unique work is created, register it with the copyright office. With Photo CD, bulk registration of images is possible, and this can result in a lower registration costs for the photographer.

Pro Photo CD offers a strong line of defense for professional photographers and photo stock agencies. The Pro Photo CD Master disc has several features designed to protect the image owner. Employing some or all of these security features not only makes it more difficult for someone to use the images without authorization, but also is proof that

Retail Stores Offer Shoppers Self-Service Kiosks

APPLICATION BRIEF

Self-service kiosks in retail stores will allow customers to search for a specific product or browse through various categories of product pictures when looking for a gift inspiration. The full color images displayed in the kiosk will come from Photo CD discs. Text descriptions and voice over the image can be part of the presentation.

The Photo CD kiosks also can be used as information kiosks for customers, directing them to the area of the store that has the product they want to buy.

Another possibility is the addition of a feature that will enable the customer to purchase a product from the kiosk and pick it up on the way out of the store.

A kiosk that might be used for Photo CD merchandising. (Courtesy Interad Corp.)

steps have been taken by the image owner to meet the legal requirements for copyright notification.

With Pro Photo CD, a professional photographer can put copyright notices on the stored digital images and also add a watermark that indicates the image is intended only to be used as a proof and not for publication or broadcast. The watermark can be a pattern or simply the word PROOF.

Encryption

Another safeguard offered by Pro Photo CD is encryption, which prevents image files from being copied off the disc without authorization. The encryption scheme is designed to enable photographers to provide a code number to their customers once the rights to use a particular image have been agreed on.

Another technique to protect image ownership is to distribute proofs on Photo CD Catalog discs, which hold only low-resolution images. When an order is placed for a digital image, it can be filled by sending a Pro Photo CD disc or by transmitting the image from that disc to the client.

Legal Remedies

When a photographer discovers that someone has used his or her work without authorization, it may be necessary to seek legal help. It is best to look for a local attorney who has specialized in copyright, trademark, or libel law. The average lawyer is not likely to be well versed in these laws.

If a lawsuit is being considered, the photographer should also take into account the time and work that will be required and how much it will cost to pursue the lawsuit. For the professional photographer or the serious freelancer, protecting their copyright is important because their livelihood is at stake. However, principle should be balanced against economics—the cost of pursuing a lawsuit to a trial court may too high.

When it comes to negotiating terms for the rights to photographs and other images, many people do not like to use their attorneys if they can avoid it. That may be penny-wise and pound-foolish, particularly if long-term arrangements are being negotiated for potentially profitable photo rights.

CHAPTER 7

The Compact Disc Family

Photo CD is part of a larger CD family. The audio CD is one of the great success stories of the past decade. Today, in stores that sell recorded music, it is hard to find anything but compact discs. A similar shift to CD is beginning in the computer marketplace. Magnetic disk drives are the standard today for data storage, but optical CDs, because of their greater capacity and lower cost, are likely to become the preferred medium in the next few years.

The computer CD-ROM disc is a natural outgrowth of the audio CD. All versions of CDs are based on specifications developed by Philips and Sony. These standards provide the definitions of the physical format of CDs. Philips and Sony have published standards for various versions of CDs for computers: CD-ROM (read only memory), CD-ROM XA (extended architecture), CD-I (interactive), and CD-WO (write-once), also called CD-W (writable) and CD-R (recordable). Once data has been recorded on any of these discs, the computer can only read the data; it cannot change or erase what is on the CD.

In addition, some manufacturers have begun marketing magneto-optical drives that can both read and record data on erasable-rewritable CD discs. Data that has been optically recorded on the disc can be erased by a strong magnetic field and new data can be written in that area by the laser beam.

Another development that combines optical and magnetic technologies are magnetic disks that have microscopic optical "servo" tracks permanently built in. These optical servo tracks make it possible to position the magnetic head of the drive much more precisely, thus allowing more tracks and more data to be recorded on the medium. These optical-magnetic drives can read standard magnetic media, but not optical CD-ROM discs.

Computer users who are working in multimedia or other applications requiring multiple images have found that CD-ROM drives and discs give them the storage capacity they need for a reasonable cost. Tandy, Apple, and other computer manufacturers offer CD-ROM drives with their computers. However, there still are conflicting standards being used for computer CD discs. The original CD-ROM has been extended to CD-ROM XA, which in turn is a bridge format to CD-I. Discs for CD-ROM XA originally had to be recorded in a single session, and the XA drive could read only a single session on a disc. Multi-session reading capability has been included in the latest generation of CD-ROM XA drives.

Compact Disc Standards

Iterations of the compact disc include CD-ROM, CD-I, and CD-WO (or CD-R) (Figure 7-1). Philips and Sony jointly hold the rights to CD technology and publish the specifications for CD products. These specifications are known by the color of the binders in which they are published. Most computer system designers are familiar with this, but not the ordinary user of CD products. To better understand CD, let's review the various specifications for CDs.

The Red Book—CD Audio
CD Digital Audio (CD-DA, or CD Audio) provides audio standards, including specifications for pulse code modulation, some error correction, control and display encoding,

Figure 7-1. Photo CD finds its origins in CD audio, but uses portions of several other standards to reach the multi-session level.

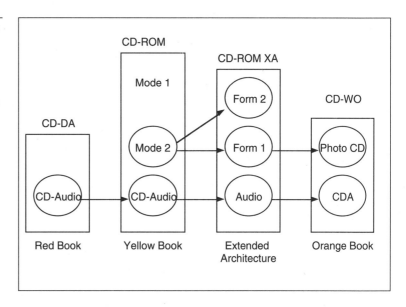

and subcode channels. Constant linear velocity (CLV) rotation is used and addressing is done by tracks.

The Red Book, published in 1980, represents an industry-wide standard to which all digital audio CDs and CD players conform. It is also the basis for allowing all other CD specifications to be compatible with previous versions.

Physically, the disc is 120 mm in diameter, with information coded in pits molded into transparent material with a specified optical refraction index. While playing, the drive mechanism holds the disc in the clamping area. Information is not recorded in this area or the outer 3 mm reserved for handling the disc.

The pits are arranged in a counter-clockwise, continuous spiral from inside to outer edge. The track pitch provides about 20,000 tracks that can hold up to seven billion bits of data. To read the disc, a focused laser beam passes through the transparent substrate layer. When the beam strikes a pit, light is reflected back from the underlying reflective layer to a photodetector (Figure 7-2).

Figure 7-2. A Photo CD disc contains a transparent substrate layer, a dye layer, a gold reflective layer, and a protective layer. A laser in the PCD writer removes dye in specific areas to make pits.

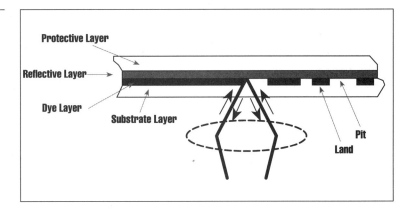

The data portion of the disc includes a lead-in with a table of contents, the program area, and a lead-out. The effects of eccentricity in rotation are corrected by a servo track that allows the player to make the necessary adjustments while reading the data on the disc.

The Yellow Book—CD-ROM

Compact discs can store any type of digital data, not just audio information. But the CD Audio format is not suitable for storing computer data because its error correction capability is not high enough to meet computer standards and because computers require direct digital output. In addition, developers need specifications for how a computer is to control the drive.

The Yellow Book standard for CD-ROM (read-only memory), published in 1984, is an adaption of the CD Audio disc standard and uses the physical format from the Red Book as a common value. The Yellow Book provides greater error detection and correction and is aimed at digital data storage. The Yellow Book uses the basic drive mechanisms and disc manufacturing processes that are specified in the Red Book.

The common physical format of CDs ensures readability on any drive. The physical compatibility of CD discs is the major difference between CD-ROM and other optical media.

CD-ROM XA

CD-ROM XA (extended architecture) is an application extension, the Microsoft Extensions, of the Yellow Book and a bridge format between CD-ROM and CD-I. The Microsoft Extensions use elements of the Green Book (CD-I) and are consistent with ISO 9660 information processing. The Microsoft Extensions (1986) introduce the concept of file types—real-time files and records including ADPCM audio and video from CD-I. This makes it possible to define a page or create a document-oriented presentation of text, graphics, images, and support multimedia.

The Green Book—CD-I

The Green Book (1987) specification describes ways of providing audio, video, graphics, text, and machine-executable code for CD-ROM, using ISO 9660 standards and CD-ROM XA specifications. It requires a player that contains a 68000-based computer with 1 megabyte of RAM, a ROM-based operating system, and real-time audio and video chips. The standard is designed to allow different manufacturers to produce CD-I players and discs that are compatible with one another.

The Orange Book—CD-WO

There are several acronyms for write-once CDs for computers. At one time the acronym was WORM (write once, read many), and that has been changed to CD-WO (write once) or just CD-W (writable). Some manufacturers prefer to use CD-R (recordable) instead of CD-W. There also are the erasable-rewritable CD discs that use a combined opto-magnetic technology.

Write-once and erasable-rewritable compact discs are considered separately in the Orange Book. CD-WO specifies a system that can be written once and read many times. The recorded CD-WO disc is compatible with the Red Book specifications, but its format allows both audio and data recording.

Unlike a typical audio disc, the CD-WO disc contains a spiral groove with a photosensitive recording layer over it. This groove is wobbled and provides timing information and motor speed control. All recording takes place in this groove.

During the recording step, the laser beam removes the dye in a tiny area of the photosensitive layer to create pits that expose the metallic reflective layer below. The reflected light is sensed by a photodetector that converts the light signals into digital data.

Orange Book specifications provide for a hybrid disc that can contain premastered or prerecorded data as well as a prepared area for recording data (Figure 7-3).

Photo CD Standards

Photo CD is based on Orange Book standards and uses the international standards ISO 9660 and 9660+ (the current appendable version of 9660). It has a block structure and supports block, track, and index table addressing. With track addressing, only track numbers are identified, not files. Block addressability, which is blind to tracks, can address image files, using ISO 9660.

To allow Photo CD discs to be read by players without expensive built-in computers, Kodak has put image access tables on the disc. Index table addressing uses a special "physical on-disc structure" to identify image files and for image file access at the beginning of the disc without having to use ISO 9660.

When a Gold Kodak disc is recorded with multi-session Image Pacs, it becomes a Photo CD disc. The same disc can can also be used to create a standard CD-ROM.

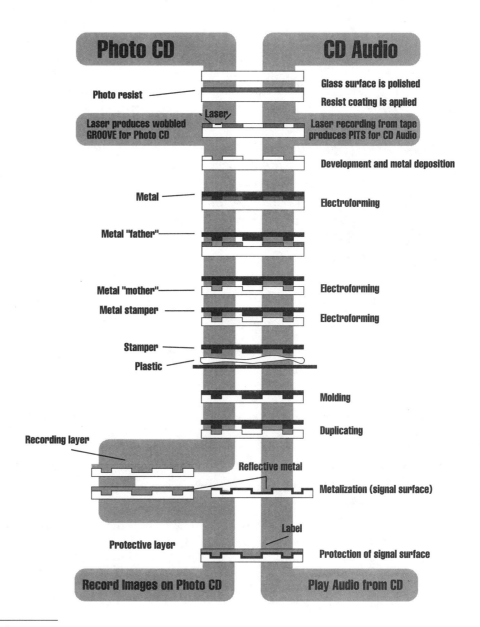

Figure 7-3. A comparison of the manufacture of a Photo CD disc (left) and an audio CD disc (right).

Photo CD as an Archive Medium

Building on Photo CD's potential for archiving high-quality photographs, Kodak has developed the Professional Photo CD Image Library to provide users with an image database system that can manage pictures in the same way that office database systems manage text (Figure 7-4).

The Professional Photo CD Image Library system is designed to meet the needs of museums, public and corporate libraries, stock photography agencies, medical and industrial photographers, and government agencies. Currently, most of these organizations maintain huge files of prints, negatives, and transparencies. Finding a particular picture in a large filing cabinet can be extremely difficult.

Figure 7-4. The Kodak Professional Photo CD Image Library stores as many as 100 Photo CD discs.

The Image Library consists of an automated disc library, or jukebox, a computer workstation with Kodak's image search retrieval software, and output devices, which can be a color printer, a film recorder, or the Kodak PCD Writer 200 for recording the image on another Photo CD disc.

The jukebox can hold as many as 100 Photo CD discs. The library accepts any of the five Photo CD disc formats. The final capacity of the jukebox depends on what Photo CD format discs are chosen. For example, the jukebox can hold 2500 4 by 5-inch film images on Kodak Pro Photo CD Master discs, 10,000 35mm images on standard Kodak Photo CD Master discs, or hundreds of thousands of the low-resolution images on Kodak Photo CD Catalog discs. A SCSI interface allows several jukeboxes to be linked or daisy-chained together when greater capacity is needed.

Using Kodak's image search and retrieval software, an operator at the workstation uses keywords to search the library. The images that fit the search criteria are displayed in low-resolution thumbnails. The system can search 10,000 thumbnail images in 10 seconds or less.

When an image is selected, the software automatically locates the appropriate Photo CD disc in the jukebox. A higher-resolution version of the image is read from the disc within a few seconds, after which it can be viewed, exported to another software program for editing, or output to a peripheral, such as a printer or film recorder. The output can be in any or all of the image resolutions stored on the Photo CD disc (Figure 7-5).

Existing picture files can be converted to Photo CD using a Photo CD workstation and scanner. After the images are scanned, they are processed by Kodak's Photo CD authoring software and recorded on either Photo CD Master or Kodak Pro Photo CD Master discs. The disc is prepared the standard way; no special formatting is required.

Next, an operator at the workstation or a desktop computer characterizes each Photo CD image with appropriate keywords that describe attributes (such as "photographer name" and "type of film") and content (such as "landscape,"

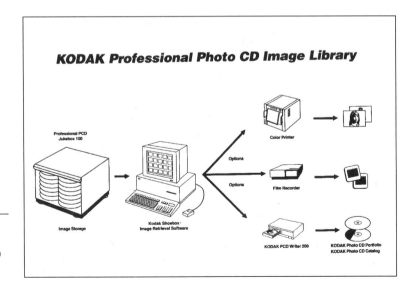

Figure 7-5. Flow diagram of the Kodak Professional Photo CD Image Library.

or "beach scene" or "corporate headquarters—exterior"). A thumbnail from the Photo CD disc and its descriptive information is then added to the image library database on the computer's hard drive, and the images are now ready for the Image Library's search and retrieval software.

Image searches do not have to be carried out from the Image Library's computer. Other computers can use networks or modems to connect the system's computer and initiate a search. The Professional Photo CD Image Library system offers on-line retrieval of any single image in a matter of seconds.

In addition, users of the Kodak Picture Exchange, the company's telephone dial-up image services network, can access the Professional Image Library system. With the Kodak Picture Exchange, which can link dozens of image databases, a user could have access to millions of images.

The capacity of the Image Library can be multiplied with the use of the Kodak Catalog CD. Each Photo CD catalog disc can contain up to 12,000 thumbnail images along with descriptive text, which can be used for image searches. And each catalog disc includes Browser software that enables the computer operator to search for images by using text descriptors.

Writing Your Own CD-ROMs

With the availability of the Kodak PCD Writer 200, it is possible to create CD-ROM discs with your own computer system. But if you want to take advantage of the Photo CD format, you must use the Kodak Photo CD authoring software. Other software for recording images and other data on CD-ROM discs is available, and several other manufacturers offer CD drives that can create a CD-ROM disc.

Although the Photo CD system was designed for storing digital images, it has a host of other potential applications when used as a standard CD-ROM. The same disc that becomes a Photo CD when it has Image Pacs recorded on it can be used as a CD-ROM.

Some companies already have adopted CD-ROM as the medium for certain operations. MCI used to send its corporate clients reams of computer printout or several reels of computer tape that listed long-distance telephone calls made by company employees. MCI now is now sending the telephone billing to its major clients on a CD-ROM disc (Figure 7-6).

This could be the forerunner of the way that large volumes of data will be distributed in the future. The data on CD-ROM discs can be in a form that lends itself to computer analysis. At MCI, the use of CD-ROM is part of its strategy to offer major clients paperless billing alternatives.

Figure 7-6. The MCI compact disc will be used with MCI Perspective, a software program that converts data into easily understood graphs, charts, and diagrams.

Another company, Meridian Data, has developed a family of publishing, networking, and multimedia applications on CD-ROMs. These CD-ROM applications have been used to create databases dealing with biomedical and chemical research, material safety, satellite imagery, the environment, and education.

Medical Records on Photo CD

APPLICATION BRIEF

Hospitals and doctors accumulate huge files of medical images that usually are stored separately from patient files. Photo CD offers a means for linking medical images with patient records in a computer.

Medical imaging includes photographs of patients, X-rays, and a variety of digital images from CT (computerized tomography), MR (magnetic resonance), and ultrasound. The Photo CD Medical format has been developed to meet the diverse needs of medical photography.

For instance, high-quality images of photomicrographs of tissues can be stored on a Photo CD disc and retrieved by computer when needed. Or a high-quality print or slide can be produced from the digital image on the disc.

Scanned images on a Medical Photo CD. (Permission to reproduce courtesy Eastman Kodak Company)

In doctor offices and smaller hospitals, the files of patients with extensive diagnostic imaging could include a Photo CD disc with all of the patients' medical images on it. In larger medical institutions, the images could be stored in Kodak's Photo CD Image Library system and retrieved by computer.

In addition to the field of medicine, Photo CDs are expected to be used as an image storage medium in other scientific fields applications such as biology, high-energy physics, astronomy, geology, and others.

Kodak Writable CD Applications

Kodak Writable CD, the recordable media, as it is sometimes referred to by people at Kodak, can be used for recording data directly from mainframes at the same time as the data is being recorded on microfilm. Or the CD can replace microfilm as the recording medium.

In other applications, Kodak Writable CD may reduce or even eliminate the need for companies to keep paper records of customer billings, insurance policies, or medical, credit, and accounting records.

The aircraft and automotive industries were some of the first users of CD-ROM. The writable CD provides a convenient means for the storage of massive amounts of data, such as that generated by oil exploration, monitoring economic activity, bank records, and government agency records. Government agencies will find many new applications for this space-saving storage technology. The CD-ROM could be used to distribute customized census data. In the commercial world, writable CD-ROMs may be used by banks to store signatures for verification. Companies with computers linked in a network could send data for recording on a writable CD in the same way they now send pages to a laser printer.

Companies like Hewlett-Packard and Sun Microsystems have already established compact discs as the medium for distributing documentation to their workstation customers. In the legal field, writable CDs could be used to store the information now in filing cabinets. Customized CD discs can put vast amounts of legal information at the lawyer's fingertips.

The future of writable CD appears to be as bright as that for Photo CD. Both offer lower cost and more efficient data storage.

Artist Portfolio

APPLICATION BRIEF

Artists can transfer slides and photographs of their work to Photo CD discs to create a permanent record of their work, which often is a problem when dealing with slides or color prints, which may be lost if they are not returned. A single disc can hold 100 high-resolution full-color images that can be used for publication in art books and magazines. Photo CD images can be transmitted by modem.

Images on the disc can be used in presentations or to show clients specific examples of an artist's work. Art galleries can use Photo CD discs to show prospective clients works of art available from artists they represent and to store photographs of shows held in the gallery. Photo CD's search feature can be used to find items that are of the greatest interest to prospective clients.

Photo CD Portfolio discs could become an alternative catalog for major art shows, combining color images with descriptive text and voice. The Portfolio art catalogs can be viewed on a TV set or on a computer screen.

At the University of Southern California library, photographs from as far back as 1860 have been scanned and transferred to Photo CDs.

Art gallery owners are planning to take advantage of Photo CD. Dyansen Corp. chief executive officer Harris Shapiro said, "Only images of superior quality can elicit an appreciation of the fine art and artists showcased in our many galleries. With its Photo CD system, Eastman Kodak Company is providing an exciting new way to display and distribute works of art in an electronic format, while maintaining the image quality our business requires."

CHAPTER 8

The Future of Photo CD

The Photo CD marriage of traditional film and computer technologies promises to change the way we live, work, and play, providing new, interactive options in entertainment, education, and business.

How Photo CD develops in the future will depend not only on Kodak's efforts, but also on the efforts of the growing number of partner companies that are using and extending Photo CD technology.

At first look, Photo CD appears to be a protective measure for the makers of conventional photo products. There may be a degree of truth in that view. Conventional photo products have characteristics that cannot be matched today by digital imaging.

Digital photo imaging is in its infancy. Film photography is still a more powerful and cost-effective way to create color pictures than digital photography. This is not to say that the digital medium will not make the quantum leaps needed to join the ranks of VCRs and audio CDs in the consumer marketplace.

Photo CD has the potential of becoming the *de facto* standard for photo image storage. The principal advantages of Photo CD are the quality of the images, ease of storage, ease of recording, and ease of use in computers and on home TV sets. Walter Bender, Principal Research Scientist at the MIT Media Lab, aptly described the Photo

CD as, "More than shiny plastic, but an architecture that will work for a long, long time."

The digital qualities of Photo CD give us storage, display, and enhancement capabilities that open new paths for imagination and communication. Like all new inventions, it is difficult to visualize what Photo CD is best suited for. The transistor market boom was not born with just the invention of the transistor, but was sparked by Akio Morita's vision of a pocket-size transistor radio that launched Sony into a worldwide market.

Photo CD offers this same sense of challenge and imagination. The winners will profit from their application of Photo CD. Others will find fault with Photo CD, but they may be missing the doughnut because they are looking only at the hole.

When Kodak first developed Photo CD, to some it appeared to be little more than tomorrow's slide projector—particularly for home use. Kodak has continued to develop the Photo CD system until it now is a powerful medium that can become an essential part of the digital computer systems used in the business world. Thus, the Photo CD system can radically change the way we use photographs in both the home and business environments.

Networking

In electronic mail, there is a trend to send documents as images rather than as strings of text. The same trend is found in office computer networks, both local area networks and wide area networks. Kodak sees networking as a key digital imaging market in the future. Photographs, like electronic mail, can be sent instantly from office to office anywhere in the world.

Some of these capabilities are already in place in the networks set up for the photographs which appear in our magazines and newspapers. The strategic transmission of photographs have been important to NASA as well as in military and law enforcement intelligence.

With Photo CD, the digital photo is now available in a standard form that lends itself to compression in an optimized form in a variety of formats that meet particular needs.

Training Manuals

APPLICATION BRIEF

Many major companies are converting their training manuals into "talking slide presentations" that are stored on Photo CD discs. The discs can be easily duplicated and made available at all the office or manufacturing sites where training is required. The Photo CD discs can contain verbal explanations and graphics as well as pictures. Each Photo CD image can be viewed as long as needed, and the resolution is higher than that provided by videotape.

Photo CD discs can be produced inexpensively, which means even small companies can use them for training. Both office procedures and manufacturing procedures can be taught using the discs.

Large operations often have very large manuals that detail procedures, but are difficult to use for training. The aircraft industry has begun using Photo CD discs to replace the large printed training manuals required for each aircraft. The new "digitized" manuals offer faster access to needed information.

Kodak Picture Exchange

With the introduction of the Kodak Picture Exchange, Kodak has taken a significant step in creating a global network for receiving and transmitting color images.

The high quality of Pro Photo CD images, and their digital format, has opened the opportunity for transmitting images more freely. The Kodak Picture Exchange (KPX) is a cooperative, on-line service designed to allow immediate access to image database (Figure 8-1).

After connecting to KPX via modem, users have search access to a textual database. Search "hits" are shown as thumbnail images on the user's screen. When an image is selected, the system will tell you who the image belongs to and how to order the image.

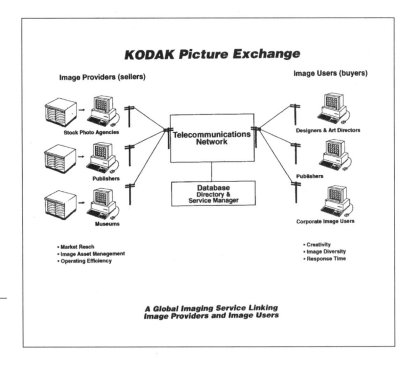

Figure 8-1. The Kodak Picture Exchange (KPX)

Kodak Picture Exchange represents the company's vision for a global imaging services network, similar to the commercial information networks like CompuServe. Kodak Picture Exchange will link distributors of images, such as stock photo houses, with customers they serve, including graphic designers and publishers.

As with conventional on-line services, Kodak Picture Exchange will allow people to use a modem for access from their desktop computers. Image users will conduct fast on-line searches using keywords and will review low-resolution thumbnail images. After images have been chosen, Kodak Picture Exchange alerts the image suppliers. In most cases, it is expected that Photo CD discs, prints, negatives, or transparencies will be sent within hours by express delivery.

Qualified image providers will be able to post on Kodak Picture Exchange any image that has been converted to a standard Photo CD digital format. Each image will be stored on the network in a low-resolution "thumbnail" form and will be linked to a descriptive index to aid in its retrieval. This index could include the photographer's name, ownership information, as well as keywords that describe the subject and attributes of the picture.

Software used to search Kodak Picture Exchange is similar to Kodak's Shoebox image-retrieval software. In other words, Kodak Picture Exchange will share a common interface with other Photo CD image databases that run Shoebox software and the Kodak Professional Photo CD Image Library. This provides a consistent look and feel and common user interface.

Image providers and users will be asked to pay nominal annual membership fees to join Kodak Picture Exchange. In addition, image providers will be charged an annual per-image storage fee and a referral fee for each hard copy image request fulfilled for a customer.

In the future, the system will handle complete order fulfillment as well. Initially, because of the limit of transmission capabilities of telephone lines, images will be sent by overnight couriers in the format the customer requests. In the future, as improved communications occurs, the images may be electronically transmitted to customers.

This same approach may be viable for images intended for home use. The pictures of grandparents or children may be sent over future phone lines to distant family members or to photofinishers.

Kodak's Relationships

Kodak has established relationships with several key manufacturers in the computer and photography industries. Besides the numerous software and hardware vendors whose products support Photo CD, certain companies have made a strategic commitment to the technology.

Apple Computer

Apple Computer has incorporated direct access to Photo CD images in its QuickTime architecture. This will give Macintosh computer users the ability to add Photo CD digital images to slide presentations, documents, multimedia presentations, and any application that can be enhanced with the use of images.

In addition, major vendors of Macintosh applications software have introduced, or will soon introduce, new software versions that read Photo CD images directly. Kodak and Fuji Photo both plan to use Apple Macintosh computers as imaging workstations.

Novell

Kodak and Novell, a leading networking vendor, will work to build system software that will extend the capability of Novell's NetWare system to process images across local-area and enterprise-wide networks. The extended NetWare will provide a foundation for independent software vendors and value-added-resellers to offer network imaging applications.

Kodak's Desktop Document Imaging (DDI) Group will work with Novell to develop image processing, mass storage, and object management technology to add to NetWare. Kodak will also provide Novell with application programming interfaces, and NetWare loadable module (NLM) tools that will allow systems and applications to handle images more efficiently on NetWare networks. The software services from Kodak will be tightly coupled with NetWare's operating system and provide open platform support for front-end applications, database products, and NLMs.

NetWare network server operating system software integrates desktop computers, servers, minicomputers, and mainframe platforms for information sharing. Novell's NetWare computing products manage and control the sharing of services, data, and applications among PC workgroups, departmental networks, and business-wide information systems. NetWare products support standards to integrate desktop computers running DOS, OS/2, Windows, Macintosh, and UNIX operating systems with each other and with IBM, DEC, and UNIX hosts.

Kodak's Desktop Document Imaging technology encompasses a robust set of imaging services that can be added to desktop applications. Kodak is delivering its image software to major hardware, software, and network vendors.

Lotus Development

In April 1991, Eastman Kodak and Lotus Development Corporation entered a strategic relationship to add advanced imaging capabilities to Lotus Notes, a group-communications software product for networked personal computers. Under the terms of the agreement, Kodak's document image processing technology, including image capture, storage, and management, will be developed as a Lotus Notes add-on product. When installed with Notes, the add-on will allow images to be integrated into any Notes application.

Lotus Notes is used for a variety of applications including customer and client tracking, discussions, document libraries, and newswire service. Users have stated that Notes has fundamentally changed the way their people work together, improving time to marketing and organizational effectiveness.

Kodak's View of Photo CD

Eastman Kodak sees Photo CD as a transition from film to digital images. Its initial efforts were directed to developing a consumer product for home use, but it soon found that people in the computer industry, particularly those involved with desktop publishing applications, were expressing great interest in the product. It soon became apparent that there were great opportunities for Photo CD in business, industrial, commercial, medical, and publishing fields.

Eastman Kodak conducted extensive consumer surveys in the United States, England, and Germany and was able to draw several important conclusions about Photo CD and viewing images on TV, according to Peter M. Palermo, Kodak's Consumer Imaging vice president and general manager.

"Traditional silver-halide photography will continue as the cornerstone of current and future imaging platforms," he noted. "But we firmly believe that hybrid electronic imaging systems will play an increasingly important, synergistic role in the growth of our industry. And we're not alone in that belief.

"First, consumers liked the superb quality of Photo CD images. Second, they liked seeing their favorite pictures on television, the convenient access, the large image, and the opportunity to share with others. Third, they liked easy and compact storage of their images; no sorting and digging through envelopes and mini-albums. And, fourth, they liked the concept of the Photo CD player's dual use playback, both for high quality music and pictures.

"This survey confirmed the strong and broad mass market appeal of Photo CD. We can ride the wave of the compact disc format, where CDs and CD players are experiencing the fastest household penetration of any consumer product in history.

"A digital imaging system that complements conventional photography can be leveraged by labs who are well-versed in serving customers' imaging needs, supported by participation of major manufacturers of film, cameras, computer hardware and software."

This is how David A. Lehman, director of strategic planning for Kodak's information sector sees Kodak's role in color imaging: "From the first color photographs to the introduction of color in motion pictures, color images have long been proven to communicate more powerfully than black-and-white. Drawing on our long history of leadership in color imaging, Kodak is demonstrating the ability to bring the power of color images to the world of desktop computing. From capture to image management to color output, Kodak has used its expertise to make color imaging a viable option for today's offices."

The professional photography industry stands poised on the threshold of a change of near revolutionary proportions, according to David P. Biehn, vice president and general manager of Kodak Professional Imaging. The challenge facing professionals in the photographic industry is to take advantage of current revolutionary technological changes by being an agent of change, rather than a victim of it.

"What I am talking about is a new world where silver and silicon meet," said Biehn. "Where traditional photographic images still mean quality, but where electronics and digital imaging mean value and additional freedom and accessibility for the users of photographic images."

To survive in this new world, Biehn urged professionals to first, re-examine their business, its purpose, and its ability to not only respond to but to master change. Next, to be attentive to market shifts and changes, finding ways to exploit and explore creative market niches. And finally, to identify their involvement in the resolution of technological change.

Biehn stressed the importance of strategic intent. "Strategic intent is an integrative approach," he explained. "You might begin with an understanding of what your competitive skills are, the creativity you bring to the job, and your resourcefulness. It is also about knowing the markets you need to serve and understanding the customers within each of them.

"The world of digital imaging is here and we at Kodak are committed to working with the industry to help explore and navigate that new world. We can navigate these changing waters by working together, by attending to the need of our customers, and by mastering the new technology. In so doing, we will not only manage change, we will thrive on it. And, I believe, we will discover—and capture—a future with a world of opportunities."

That's the view of a few of the people at Kodak—a view shared by many leaders in the photo industry.

"Digital" Slide Shows for Presentations and Lectures

APPLICATION BRIEF

Photo CDs offer the opportunity of creating "digital" shows with photographs, graphs, text, and even audio. Video projectors allow the projection of images suitable for small or theater-sized audiences.

Photo CDs can be used instead of slides or overhead transparencies to illustrate a lecture or talk. Instead of having to carry slides and arrange them individually in slide carousels, speakers can carry Photo CD discs, which are small enough to be put in a pocket or purse. The Photo CD discs can have programmed sequences, or speakers can choose to select images as they talk, or interrupt a sequence to branch to additional pictures.

Business presentations can be dramatically enhanced using a television or computer screen to display images from Photo CD discs. Specific products or illustrations can be quickly retrieved in response to clients queries. The relevant product pictures and information can be later output on a color printer and sent to the client, or the information can be transmitted by electronic mail directly to the client's computer.

Kodak CEO Kay Whitmore used a Photo CD and Photo CD player to illustrate a recent talk.

Instead of slides, Kay Whitmore, chief executive officer of Eastman Kodak Company, used a Photo CD and a standard Photo CD player to illustrate a talk he gave to a Human Resource Planning Society Conference. None of the audience suspected that they were not watching the usual slide show. The first any member of the audience knew that the talk was not on conventional slides was when Whitmore held up the gold-colored disc and let the audience in on the secret.

Welcome to Tomorrow

Welcome to the world of the Photo CD and welcome to the emerging world of the digital image. Photo CD is here today—a natural bridge to the digital world—a world combining silver and silicon. Will there be a day when all will be a digital world? Yes, but with Photo CD we have the means for making a smooth transition while using the best of both worlds.

Try Photo CD—you'll like it.

Interior Design and Furniture Showcase

APPLICATION BRIEF

An easy way for interior designers to show different paints, carpet, and furniture treatments is with Photo CDs. The random access capabilities of the Photo CD player lets the designer move to areas that meet customer expectations and preferences. Interior designers can show their Photo CDs in the client's home or office. Furniture manufacturers can show customers their full line of products using Photo CDs. Images on the Photo CD disc also can be used by the manufacturer or furniture store in newspaper, television, and magazine advertisements.

Furniture from a Photo CD catalog disc. (Permission to reproduce courtesy Eastman Kodak Company.)

Image Storage and Directories

Images are stored on a Photo CD disc in a region called an Image Pac. Image Pacs are stored on the disc in sequential order, starting with the first image transferred to the disc (Figure A-1).

Every Photo CD disc also contains an Overview Pac, a copy from the Image Pacs of all the Base/16 images currently on the disc, collected into one location.

Figure A-1. The structure of Image Pac data.

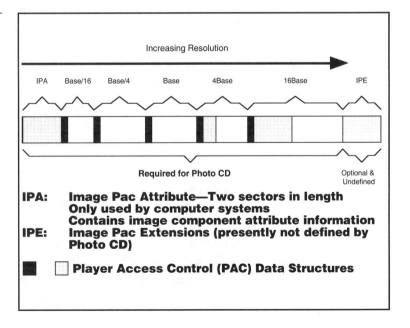

Photo CD File Structure

Images are stored and organized on a Photo CD disc as a file system with a hierarchical directory structure, to make them accessible and convenient for computer use.

Each disc contains a directory called PHOTO_CD, which in turn contains a directory called IMAGES, the Overview Pac, and other ancillary information files. The IMAGES directory contains an Image Pac file for each image on the Photo CD disc. The names of individual Image Pac files include image numbers that correspond to those on the index print (Figure A-2).

The root directory, O, may contain subdirectories, in addition to those shown above, that enable the addition to the Photo CD disc of other data files.

Photo CD System file-naming conventions significantly restrict character use, so that file names may be used in the widest variety of operating systems and international environments. A valid name includes a 1- to 8-character file name and an optional 3-character extension. The file name and extension must be selected from 37 characters—numeric digits, uppercase letters, and the underscore—in the International Reference Version of ISO 646.

Images can be added to a Photo CD disc in several sessions. To increase compatibility with existing CD-ROM systems, the Photo CD System uses the international standard ISO 9660:1988 Logical Volume and File Structure of CD-ROM for Information Interchange, for those Image Pacs that are within the first session of a disc.

Higher order sessions of a Photo CD disc are similar to the first session, except CD-WO Volume and File Structures are used instead of the current ISO 9660:1988. Only newer-

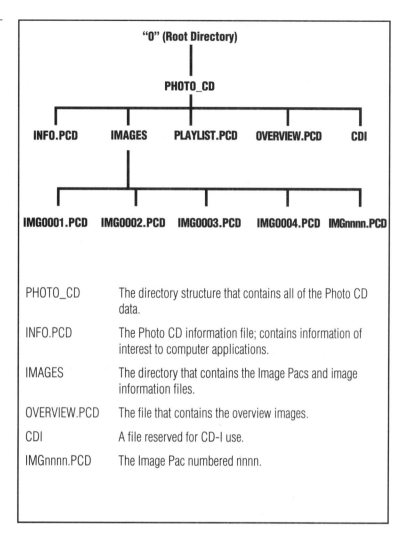

PHOTO_CD	The directory structure that contains all of the Photo CD data.
INFO.PCD	The Photo CD information file; contains information of interest to computer applications.
IMAGES	The directory that contains the Image Pacs and image information files.
OVERVIEW.PCD	The file that contains the overview images.
CDI	A file reserved for CD-I use.
IMGnnnn.PCD	The Image Pac numbered nnnn.

generation systems will be able to access the additional sessions of a multi-session disc.

Eastman Kodak Company and N.V. Philips designed the Photo CD disc structure to work in a broad range of customer environments. The disc structure combines the attributes of CD audio, CD-ROM, and interactive CD (CD-I) with the attributes of writable CDs.

Photo CD discs contain certain data structures that provide efficient image access and display by the Photo CD players. Additional data structures permit image access and display in computer environments equipped with hardware compatible with CD-ROM XA readers.

The Photo CD System takes advantage of the capabilities of the XA environment by using a Mode 2 Form 1 sector structure from the Sony/Philips "Green Book." This structure makes Photo CD discs compatible with CD-I and other systems that use the Mode 2 format.

To allow data to be added to a Photo CD disc—yet retain compatibility with low-cost players—the Photo CD System uses a hybrid disc, as described in the Sony/Philips "Orange Book." A hybrid disc has multiple program areas called sessions. Hybrid-disc technology also enables Photo CD discs to be premastered as single-session discs.

Adding Images to an Existing Photo CD

When a customer wants images added to a Photo CD disc that already contains images, the additional digitized images are appended in a subsequent session. A session is completed when it is bracketed by lead-in and lead-out tracks; this uses about 18MB of the Photo CD storage space. The disc is then ready to return to the customer, who can play it in a Photo CD player.

All images from all sessions can be displayed using a Photo CD player. Likewise, all images in all sessions are accessible from an XA-compatible computer system configured with the appropriate hardware and software to recognize hybrid discs.

Each session on a Photo CD disc contains data structures that are associated with the different elements of the Photo CD System. As with Image Pacs, each session incorporates data structures specifically for use by consumer players, computer operating systems, and computer applications.

To locate images on the disc, the consumer player uses the Index Table structure. The Index Table contains disc identification information, pointers to Photo CD Image Pacs, and other information that the consumer player uses to determine how to display the image.

To identify the volume and provide directory information, computer operating systems reference data structures defined by ISO 9660:1988. Ancillary information files, such as INFO.PCD, provide application programs with information about images on the disc.

Following these data structures are the Image Pacs. Because all Image Pacs are contiguous data structures (except if Mode 2 interleaved data are present), they are recorded as a single File Section. An Image Pac cannot cross a track boundary. Image Pacs do not contain any associated Extended Attribute Records as defined in ISO 9660:1988.

The start location of each Image Pac is the logical block number of the first logical block of the Image Pac Attribute (IPA) section of the Image Pac. For the Overview Pac, the start location is the first logical block of the Overview Pac Attribute (OPA) section. The logical block size is 2048 bytes.

When a new session is written to the Photo CD disc, new directory structures and ancillary information files that supersede the previous ones are written to the disc. The directory hierarchy in appended sessions has the same structure as that of the first session. The latest directory hierarchy describes all recorded files in all sessions of the disc. Ancillary information files such as INFO.PCD and OVERVIEW.PCD contain updated information about all sessions on the disc.

The Photo CD System requires the use of specific addressing and recording methods to increase compatibility with a variety of existing CD systems. A Photo CD Image Pac is accessed through a sector-addressing method that is used by CD-ROM discs and complies with ISO/IEC 10149:1989.

The authoring station records a disc by using the Track-at-Once recording mode described in the Sony/Philips "Orange Book." This technique introduces Sync-gaps at the start of each track. In addition, each track is bracketed by corresponding run-in, link, and run-out sectors. The overall effect of this technique is that unused sectors will exist beginning at two sectors before the end of the track, up to the first sector after the Sync-gap.

Photo CD Milestones

September 1990

Eastman Kodak Company announces the Kodak Photo CD system, the first cost-effective tool for digitally storing and manipulating photographs. The system will allow consumers to store their pictures in a new way and view them on television. It will bring photographic quality 35mm color or black-and-white photos into computer applications at a reasonable cost.

October 1990

Kodak announces a series of developments designed to make it easy to bring Photo CD images to computer applications:

The Photo CD Access Developer's Toolkit, to enable software and hardware developers to integrate Photo CD technology into new and existing applications.

Photo CD Access software, a package designed to give users access to Photo CD images in computer applications that were not specifically designed with Photo CD capability.

The ColorSense color management system, a set of tools and utilities that provide consistent, high-quality color across a variety of software applications, computer platforms, and peripheral devices.

The Photo CD system is supported or endorsed by major developers of computer hardware and software, including

Adobe Systems, Apple Computer, IBM Corporation, and Sun Microsystems, all computer industry leaders.

At Photokina, in Germany, Photo CD players are shown to the public for the first time, generating enormous excitement and support from trade and consumer magazines.

November 1990
Popular Science selects the Photo CD system for a "Best of What's New" award, honoring the year's 100 greatest achievements in science and technology.

June 1991
Kodak releases its "Planning Guide for Developers," a technical overview of the Photo CD system for other companies that want to develop products based on Photo CD technology.

August 1991
Kodak announces that the Photo CD system has received two key European honors: the "Best Design Technology" award from the Technical Image Press Association, and a "Top 10 Products" award from PhotoExpo 91.

September 1991
Fuji Photo Film Company announces that it will license Photo CD technology from Kodak, thus enabling affiliated photofinishing laboratories to provide services for copying film-based images onto Photo CD discs (beginning in the fall of 1992).

Philips Interactive Media Systems announces plans to market dedicated Photo CD players beginning in the summer of 1992. Philips' CD-I players also will be Photo CD compatible.

The Photo CD system is named "European Innovation of the Year 1991-1992" by a panel of editors of photographic journals from 13 countries.

October 1991

Kodak and Intel Corporation announce support for PhotoYCC, the color encoding scheme used in the Kodak Photo CD system, on Intel's ActionMedia II boards, making it easier and faster to incorporate high-resolution images in desktop applications.

December 1991

Kodak and MCI Telecommunications announce that MCI will use Kodak recordable data CDs to deliver complex long distance bills to its largest customers, beginning in 1992. This is the first commercial application for CD technology developed by Kodak to support the introduction of the Photo CD system.

January 1992

Kodak and Agfa-Gevaert announce that Agfa will support the Kodak Photo CD system, licensing Photo CD technology from Kodak. Agfa will use Photo CD images as one source of input to the Agfa Digital Print System (DPS).

Kodak announces that the Photo CD system will offer interactive capability when it hits the market during the summer of 1992. Among other things, the new features will allow people to combine sound, text, and graphics with images, and to use branching to interact with the contents of their Photo CD discs.

Photo CD Access Developer's Toolkit availability is announced at MacWorld.

February 1992

Kodak releases details on the Photo CD Imaging Workstation (PIW) at the PMA Show.

March 1992

Kodak and Apple Computer Inc. announce that they are working together to integrate support for Photo CD images into future versions of Apple's QuickTime system software extension. QuickTime support for Photo CD images will provide Apple customers with direct access to Photo CD images within any Macintosh application.

Kodak announces that leading CD-ROM drive manufacturers Philips, Pioneer, Sony, and Toshiba will offer fully Photo CD-compatible CD-ROM XA drives. Drives that are certified by Kodak as fully Photo CD-compatible can carry the Photo CD logo.

April 1992
Kodak begins delivering Kodak Photo CD Imaging Workstations to wholesale photofinishers, commercial photo labs, and photo retail stores. Delivery of PIWs meets the target set in September 1990, when Kodak first announced it would introduce the Photo CD system.

May 1992
Eastman Kodak Company announces that it will supply a digital print scanner by year-end as an accessory to the Kodak Photo CD Imaging Workstation (PIW). The scanner will be produced with the Kodak brand by Polaroid through an OEM agreement with Kodak.

July 1992
Kodak's Stephen Stepnes and Scott Brownstein win the Eduard-Rhein Foundation's 1992 Technology Award, one of Europe's most celebrated technology prizes.

August 1992
Photo CD players are available to consumers in North America, followed by Western Europe, Japan, and other major markets.

Kodak Photo CD Access software is shipped for Apple Macintosh and Windows applications. Kodak also announces that it will market a newly Photo CD enabled Kodak Renaissance design software program.

Kodak announces a dramatically expanded Photo CD program that cuts across professional and commercial markets. The announcements include:

- Kodak Picture Exchange—a global image transmission network

- Four new Photo CD formats—Kodak Pro Photo CD Master, Photo CD Portfolio, Photo CD Catalog, and Photo CD Medical

- Kodak Professional Photo CD Imaging Workstation 4200—for large-format professional films, with features that answer professional photographers' unique needs

- Kodak Photo CD Imaging Workstation 2400—with over three times the productivity of the existing PIW, for photofinishing labs

- Four new Kodak imaging software packages—Kodak PhotoEdge, Shoebox, Browser, and Photo CD-enabled Renaissance.

Kodak also announced that more than a dozen companies will cooperate on the development of new products and commercial applications for Photo CD and Kodak Picture Exchange products and services. These included Applied Graphic Technologies (AGT), Apple Computer, Inc., J. Paul Getty Art History Information Program, Jostens, and Sony Corporation of America.

September 1992

Kodak exhibits authoring software for interactive Photo CD features at Photokina '92 in Cologne, Germany.

Glossary

Access Time. The time required for a memory device to locate and retrieve a specific piece of information.

ADC. See Analog to Digital Converter.

Additive Color System. A color system based on the three primary colors of light: red, green, and blue. All other colors are made by mixing primary colors.

Album Pages. The print pages generated by the thermal printer. The PTS Application software allows the operator to produce album pages containing a single 8-inch x 10-inch image, two 5-inch x 7-inch images, four 4-inch x 5-inch images, or up to four 3.5-inch x 5-inch images.

Aliasing. A video defect introduced when samples of an image are taken too infrequently to provide an accurate record of an event.

Analog Recording. A method of recording in which the recorded signal continuously matches the original signal in some characteristic, such as amplitude or frequency.

Analog Signal. A continuous electrical signal that varies in amplitude or frequency in response to changes in sound, light, heat, position, or pressure.

Analog to Digital Converter (ADC). A circuit that

converts continuous analog signals to digital (pulse type) signals.

Application Software. A software program designed for a specific use (such as budgeting or playing games).

Archival Storage. Permanent file storage of information.

Artifact. Visible or audible extraneous information in a signal that results in a defect in the image or sound.

Aspect Ratio. The horizontal size of an image divided by its vertical size. A conventional NTSC picture television picture is 4 units wide by 3 units high, giving it an aspect ratio of 4/3. It also may be expressed as 4:3 or "four to three."

Bandwidth. The difference between the highest and lowest frequencies of a signal. The greater the bandwidth of a transmission channel, the more information it can carry. Bandwidth is usually expressed in Hertz, or cycles per second.

Base Resolution. The image resolution (NTSC) currently displayed on consumer televisions.

> *Base/4 Resolution.* An image resolution that has 1/4 the number of pixels as the Base Resolution.

> *Base/16 Resolution.* An image resolution that has 1/16 the number of pixels as the Base Resolution.

> *4 Base Resolution.* An image resolution that has 4 times the number of pixels as the Base Resolution. This resolution is typically displayed on High Definition Televisions (HDTV).

16 Base Resolution. An image resolution that has 16 times the number of pixels as the Base Resolution.

Baud Rate. A measure of the rate at which information is transmitted. The baud rate of a communications device determines the number of bits per second (BPS) that can be transmitted.

Bit. Abbreviation for Binary Digit. A bit is the smallest unit of data in a computer system. Each bit is represented by a 1 or a 0 in binary code and represented in a computer by an "on" or "off" electronic pulse.

Bit-mapped. Images formed by a series of dots. See also Raster, Vector.

Bits Per Second (BPS). A measurement of the speed of information transmission: the number of bits of information transmitted in one second.

Bit Rate. The number of bits transmitted in a set period of time. Usually expressed in bits per second.

Bug. An error or defect that causes a program or device to function improperly. In a computer system, a hardware bug is a defect or error in the equipment; a software bug is an error in the software program.

Byte. Pronounced "bite." A sequence of adjacent bits operated on as if they were a single unit.

Cathode Ray Tube (CRT). A television or monitor tube that uses an electron gun to generate beams of electrons. These electrons illuminate specific phosphors on the screen to produce an image. In color sets, the phosphors are red, green, and blue.

CCD. See Charge Coupled Device.

CD. An acronym for compact disc. See also Photo CD.

CDTV (R) Commodore Dynamic Total Vision. A proprietary system made by Commodore International. Audio, graphics, and video images are recorded on CDTV discs, and a CDTV player is used to play back the sound and images on a computer system or TV.

CD-E. See Compact Disc-Erasable.

CD-G. See Compact Disc Graphics.

CD-I. See Compact Disc-Interactive.

CD-R. See Compact Disc-Recordable.

CD-ROM. See Compact Disc Read-Only-Memory.

CD-ROM Drive. A disc drive that is capable of reading information from a CD.

CD-ROM XA Drive. A disc drive used with personal computers that allows information stored on CDs to be accessed. The CD-ROM XA disc drives permit both audio and video capability. XA is the acronym for eXtended Architecture.

CD-WO. See Compact Disc-Write Once.

CD-W. See CD-Writable.

Central Processing Unit (CPU). The "brain" of a computer; contains internal storage, processing, and control circuitry.

CGM. See Computer Graphic Metafile.

Charge-Coupled Device (CCD). A device used to convert light into an electronic signal.

Chroma Resolution. The amount of color detail available on a monitor or television, separate from any brightness detail.

Chrominance. The difference between two colors that are equal in brightness. Reference colors are specified for comparison purposes.

CMYK. An acronym for Cyan-Magenta-Yellow-blacK used in 4-color printing process.

Color Fringing. Video distortion characterized by ragged separations between contrasting colors along the boundaries of objects in an image. Also called fringing.

Comb Filter. A filter that separates the chrominance and luminance information in a signal.

Compact Disc (CD). A plastic disc used to store music saved as digital codes. A laser-equipped player is used to read and play back the information.

Compact Disc-Erasable (CD-E). A compact disc that can be recorded and erased.

Compact Disc-Graphics (CD-G). A music CD plus graphics. In addition to 16-bit audio code, the disc has subcodes that carry textual information (such as liner notes, lyrics and pixilated, computer-like graphics). A player with the proper adaptor (possibly built-in) is needed to access the subcode information.

Compact Disc-Interactive (CD-I). A well-defined computer system in conjunction with a CD-ROM XA disc that allows the user to interact with the program by responding to prompts generated by the software. It can be used to present a series of still images for animation-like effects, along with sound effects. CD-Is are not generally considered to be a computer peripheral, but rather, a component of a home entertainment center.

Compact Disc-Read Only Memory (CD-ROM). A compact disc that stores large quantities of information in read-only format. Particularly useful for storing graphic images due to the large memory requirements of graphic storage. CD-ROM is considered a computer peripheral.

Compact Disc-Recordable. Same as Compact Disc-Write Once.

Compact Disc-Writable. Same as Compact Disc-Write Once.

Compact Disc-Write Once (CD-WO). A compact disc designed to be filled with information by the consumer.

Composite Signal. The television signal that consists of the video signal (luminance and chrominance), burst signal, and sync signal (horizontal and vertical).

Compression. A technique computers use to reduce the size of a data file, thereby reducing the amount of disk space required to store the data file.

Computer Graphic Metafile. A file format used for storing computer graphics. Images are stored primarily in vector form but CGM provides for raster format also.

Continuous-Tone Imaging. Reproduction of the original scene by producing nearly continuous amounts of cyan, magenta, and yellow dyes in subtractive systems such as prints, or continuous control of red, green, and blue luminance such as CRT displays.

CPU. See Central Processing Unit.

CRT. See Cathode Ray Tube.

DAC or D/AC. See Digital to Analog Converter.

Data Compression. The use of a coding technique to reduce the volume of stored data.

Decibel (dB). A numerical expression of the relative loudness of a sound or the relative differences in the power levels of electrical signals.

Definition. The degree of detail or sharpness of a video signal.

Desktop Publishing. A system of using a computer to lay out and typeset a publication.

Digital. Description of information encoded as a series of discrete electrical pulses based on a binary coding system (1 or 0).

Digital to Analog Converter (DAC or D/AC). A system that converts digital (discrete) signals to analog (continuous) signals.

Digitization. The process of changing an analog signal into a digital (discrete) signal.

Discrete Sampling. The process of taking separate samples and quantizing them so that an image or sound can be represented as either an analog or digital signal.

Dithering. The eye performing color blending. Also describes a method for generating halftones on a digital output device in which dots are clustered into halftone cells.

Dye Sublimation. A computer printing technology capable of producing photographic-quality images.

Edge Enhancement. The processing of an image to increase its sharpness by eliminating artifacts (extraneous information) introduced when the image was recorded.

Electronic Still Camera (ESC). A camera that contains a CCD sensor that captures and records images electronically.

Encryption. Scrambling of a signal so that the receiver must "de-scramble" it for proper reception. Encryption is considered important for signal security and pay-TV.

Field. One complete vertical scan of an image. In America, two scans are required to gather all the data required to produce the complete image. Therefore, a field is one-half of a television picture (every other horizontal line), or frame.

Field Frequency. In television, the number of frames per second times the number of fields per frame. In the United States, the field frequency is 60 fields per second.

Film Recorder. A computer output device that produces images on photographic film. Generally used to produce slides and transparencies from files created on a computer.

Film Scanner. Equipment used to convert color negatives and slides into electronic images.

Firmware. Software that is permanently stored in ROM (Read-Only Memory) so that it cannot be altered.

Frame. In television, one complete image, made up of two fields. The American NTSC broadcast system designates a rate of 30 frames per second for TV.

Frequency. (1) The number of times that a wave repeats itself in one second. (2) The pitch of radio signal that distinguishes it from another. (3) An assigned channel on which a station can transmit a signal; e.g., FM 99.5.

Glitch. Unexpected random occurrence in a system.

Graphical User Interface (GUI). A software system that uses small pictures known as "icons" to represent common computer operations.

Halftone Imaging. A printing process where different sized dots or patterns are used to represent a continuous-tone image.

Hard Copy. A copy that you can hold, as a print or a slide.

Hard Disk. A disk drive with high storage capacity. This high storage capacity is achieved by using a rigid form of magnetic media and extremely close mechanical tolerances.

Hardware. Computer equipment, as opposed to "software."

HDTV. See High Definition TeleVision.

Hertz (Hz). The unit of frequency equal to one cycle per second (cps); one kilohertz (KHz) equals 1000 cps; one megahertz (MHz) equals 1,000,000 cps.

High Definition Television (HDTV). High-resolution television incorporating 1000 or more horizontal lines of resolution, wide aspect ratio, and digital quality audio.

Horizontal Resolution. A rating of the fine detail of a TV picture, measured in lines. The more lines, the higher the resolution and the better the picture. A standard TV or VCR produces 240 lines of horizontal resolution, while about 430 lines are possible with Super VHS machines.

Hue. Color values. Also called tint.

Huffman Coding. A data compression method used by the Kodak Photo CD System in which shorter code sequences are used to represent common values and longer code sequences are used to represent uncommon values.

Hz. See Hertz.

IC. See Integrated Circuit.

Image Data Manager. The component in the Kodak Photo CD System that performs color and density correction and data compression.

Image Enhancement. Techniques for changing a digital image so that it is more pleasing.

Image Pac. The Kodak Photo CD System data storage format that contains all the possible resolutions (Base/16 through 16 Base) of the associated image.

Image Rotation. Feature on Kodak Photo CD System that will allow the operator to change the orientation of an image (i.e., change a horizontal image to a more vertical orientation, or a vertical image to a more horizontal orientation).

Imagesetter. A high-resolution computer output device that produces text and images on resin-coated paper or film. Often used as an alternative to traditional prepress systems for producing color separations.

IMG. A standard bitmapped image format.

Index Print. A page of miniature, or "thumbnail," images that is used as a reference for the photographic images stored on a specific Photo CD Disc. Each "thumbnail" is numbered to indicate where the image is located on the Photo CD Disc.

Integrated Circuit (IC). A semiconductor circuit that has more than one transistor and other electronic components and can perform at least one complete electronic circuit function.

Interactive. A description of a system or device that allows (or requires) the person using the system to provide input or responses during the operation of the system.

Interface. Hardware or software used to connect two computer devices.

Interlace Scanning. Process of scanning every other line of an image, followed by a second scan to fill in the missing lines.

I/O. Jargon for "input/output." Refers to the information that is input into the system and the resulting information that is output by the system.

Jaggies. A term used to describe the jagged, or stair-stepped, appearance of diagonal lines in computer-generated, bit-mapped graphic images.

Jewel Case. The plastic case in which the Kodak Photo CD Discs will be packaged. Each jewel case will be labeled to aid identification and will hold index image prints showing the images stored on the Photo CD Disc.

JPEG. A standardized method for compressing and de-compressing still images. Short for Joint Photographic Experts Group, an organization of hardware and software developers that established the standard.

KB. See KiloByte.

KHz. See Kilohertz.

Kilobyte (KB). 1024 bytes of data. The memory capacity, especially RAM, of a computer device is generally described in terms of "K's."

Kilohertz (KHz). Thousands of cycles per second. Also known as Kilocycles.

LAN. See Local Area Network.

Laser. A device for converting light energy of various frequencies into a concentrated beam of energy with a single frequency and phase.

Laserdisc(R). A 12-inch optical disc that stores video images and sound using an analog format. Movies are released on Laserdisc(R) for the high-end market.

Laser Beam. A tightly focused beam of laser light used to record or play the signals stored on laser video discs or CD recordings.

LED. See Light Emitting Diode.

Light-Emitting Diode (LED). A small electronic device that emits light while conducting electrical current.

Linear Array. A line of CCD sensors mounted side-by-side.

Linear Array Scanning. Process of scanning line-by-line using a linear array.

Lines of Resolution. A method of describing the clarity of video image. The higher the number of the lines of resolution, the better the television picture you see.

Liquid Crystal. A semi-liquid gelatin-like crystal of organic molecules.

Liquid Crystal Display (LCD). A display composed of a thin layer of liquid crystal material between polarizing glass plates. Electricity passing through the display causes some areas of the crystal to block light, forming dark characters.

Local-Area Network (LAN). Several microcomputers that can exchange information directly using their own dedicated transmission lines.

Lossless. A form of image compression that offers a relatively limited degree of compression, but does not sacrifice any image data.

Lossy. A form of image compression that offers a high degree of compression, but that also sacrifices some image data in the process.

Luma. See luminance.

Luminance. Brightness or overall light intensity.

Luminance Signal. A video signal carrying luminance information. Its amplitude varies with the brightness of the image transmitted. Also called the Y-signal.

MB. See Megabyte.

Megabyte (MB). 1024 Kilobytes (approximately one million bytes).

Memory Card. An electronic circuit board containing memory chips to store large amounts of digital data.

Megahertz (MHz). One million Hertz. A unit of frequency equal to one million cycles per second.

MHz. See Megahertz.

Microcomputer. See Personal Computer.

Microprocessor. The main processing chip inside a computer or electronic device.

Monitor. A display device that makes the output of a computer or other device visible on a TV-like screen. Monitors are essentially televisions without tuner mechanisms.

Monochrome. Single color, usually used to indicate black and white.

Multi-Disc Changer. A feature on CD players that allows several CDs to be loaded into the player at one time.

National Television Standards Committee (NTSC). Standard television broadcasting system used in the United States; it produces 330 lines of horizontal resolution on the TV screen, providing the TV has a comb filter.

Non-Interlace Scanning. A digital-based process used in some newer high-end television sets to produce a sharper picture; this process transmits each line in sequence rather than transmitting odd and even lines in separate scans.

NTSC. See National Television Standards Committee.

Optical Disc. A non-magnetic recording disc that is written to and read using a laser beam.

Output. Data that comes out of a computer device; also, a video or audio signal that is emitted from a system.

Overscanning. Scanning more of an image than can be displayed.

PAL. See Phase Alternation by Line.

PCM. See Pulse Code Modulation.

PCX. An industry standard paint format for MS-DOS machines.

Parallel. Description of a particular computer interface; used mainly for printers.

Peripheral. A piece of equipment that is connected to a computer (CPU) and controlled by it, but that is external to it; for example, a printer or a scanner.

Personal Computer. A computer that has all the hardware and software necessary to complete one or more computing tasks, a stand-alone computer system.

Phase Alternation By Line (PAL). A common composite color transmission system used in Europe for televisions.

Phosphor. The substance on a TV or computer monitor that is illuminated when an electron beam strikes it.

Photo CD Discs. A compact disc that contains digitized, high resolution images that were originally recorded on 35mm format film.

Photo CD Scanner. The component of the Kodak Photo CD System that scans, or reads across, a film frame and digitizes the image so that it can be stored on a Photo CD Disc. The Kodak Photo CD Scanner will perform a low-resolution scan for image orientation verification, then a high-resolution scan for final digitization and storage.

Pickup. A device that converts a sound or an image into corresponding electric signals.

PICT. A graphics file format developed by Apple Computer that can accommodate vector or raster images. PICT2 supports color.

Pit. An area of high reflectance on a CD.

Pixel. A measure of resolution that refers to the smallest picture element in a digitized graphic.

Port. A computer connector (to plug in printers, game controllers, etc.).

PostScript. A page description language developed by Adobe Systems that enhances the ability of printers and other output devices to produce text and graphics.

Primary Color. A color that cannot be mixed from other colors. All non-primary colors can be mixed from primary colors. Red, green, and blue are additive primary colors; cyan, magenta, and yellow are subtractive primary colors.

Pulse Code Modulation. A technique for digitizing sound into binary code by sampling.

Quantization. The process of converting of an analog pixel brightness to a digital quantity.

Quantized Levels. The number of levels used by a data system to represent information, e.g., 1 byte (2^8) represents 256 levels. If enough quantized levels are used, the human eye cannot distinguish between the sampled image and the analog image. The Kodak Photo CD System uses this technique to reduce the amount of image data stored without sacrificing image quality.

RAM. See Random Access Memory.

RAM Card. A card that fits inside a computer that holds the RAM SIMMS.

Random Access. Describes a method of accessing information in a storage device directly, without having to scan through all previously stored material.

Random Access Memory (RAM). Computer's working memory, where data and program instructions currently being used are held.

Raster. A pattern of scanning lines that provides uniform coverage of the display. Also refers to computer images described as an array of dots. See also Vector.

Read-Only Memory (ROM). Memory that contains information that can only be read; it cannot be changed or deleted.

Real-Time. Description of computer systems that give immediate responses.

Reduced Instruction Set Computing (RISC). A computer architecture in which complex computational functions are divided into small components.

Resolution. The precision at which the smallest details in an image are portrayed. Because the Kodak Photo CD System can store and transmit more detail (in the form of electronic data) than the best monitors currently available can display, the image on the screen is extremely sharp.

RGB. An acronym for Red-Green-Blue. These are the primary colors, which are used to create full-color images in color televisions and monitors.

RISC. See Reduced Instruction Set Computer.

ROM. See Read-Only Memory.

RS-232C. Describes a specific kind of connection or port (used with serial interfaces).

Sampling. To deal with something continuous in discrete sections. The term is often used to refer to the capture of images or sounds on a computer system.

Saturation. The intensity of a color.

Scan. A device that scans the frequencies that have been programmed on all the scanner's channels.

Scanner. A computer peripheral that converts images on slides or hard copy into digital data that can be manipulated on a computer system. See also Photo CD Scanner.

Scanning. Moving of the horizontal and vertical electronic beam in a camera or TV tube. Also, reading analog data (film) with a scanner.

Scanning Line. A line that is scanned by an electron beam in order to gather one line of the information necessary to reproduce the image. More lines equal sharper images.

SECAM. Refers to a color TV system used in France and most Eastern European and Middle Eastern countries; sequential lines are scanned instead of alternate lines.

Serial. Description of a kind of interface or port used for printers, modems, and other peripherals.

Session. A single continuous occurrence of writing images to a Photo CD Disc. Typically, a transfer of one roll occurs in one session. Any subsequent appends to the disc will be another session.

Signal-to-Noise Ratio (S/N). The ratio of signal strength to the strength of unwanted, competing signals. The higher this ratio, the clearer the transmission.

S/N. See Signal-to-Noise Ratio.

Soft Display. Refers to the display of images on televisions or computer monitors, versus a paper hardcopy of the image.

Software Program. A set of instructions that guide computer operations.

Solid State. Describes an electronic device that uses semiconductors instead of vacuum tubes.

SPARC. Scalable Process Advanced RISC Computer or Scalable Performance ARChitecture. A 32-bit RISC computer developed by Sun Microsystems.

Storage Density. The amount of information that can be stored on a disk is referred to as the disk's storage density.

Store. The process of saving information.

Tagged Image File Format (TIFF). A standard file format for graphic images. TIFF files are stored in bit-mapped form and can include color.

Thermal Dye Transfer. A printing process that creates hard copies of color images by heating dyes and transferring them to a receiving paper.

Thumbnail Image. A term referring to a single, miniaturized image that appears on an index print.

TIFF. See Tagged Image File Format.

Tint. A name sometimes given to hue control on a color TV set.

Track. A band of information on a recording medium.

TV Resolution. See Base Resolution.

Vector. A category of computer graphics in which images are defined as mathematical formulas rather than an array of dots. Also referred to as "object-oriented" or "draw" graphics.

Windows. A software system developed by Microsoft Corp. that adds a graphical user interface to PC-compatible computers.

Write Once-Read Many times (WORM). Refers to electronic data storage in which the storage space on the optical disk can be written on only once; that is, once the information is stored on the disc, it cannot be edited (Write Once). However, the information on the disk can be read as many times as desired (Read Many times).

List of Manufacturers

Adobe Systems
1585 Charleston Rd.
Mountain View, CA 94039-7900
415-961-4400

Agfa Division Miles Inc.
200 Ballardvale St.
Wilmington, MA 01887
508-658-5600

Aldus Corp.
411 First Ave. So.
Seattle, WA 98104-2871
206-628-2320

Apple Computer, Inc.
20525 Mariana
Cupertino, CA 95014
408-996-1010

Astral Development Corp.
Londonderry Sq., Ste. 112
Londonderry, NH 03053
603-432-6800

Barco, Inc.
1000 Cobb Place Blvd.
Kennesaw, GA 30144
404-590-7900

CalComp Digitizers Group
14555 North 82nd St.
Scottsdale, AZ 85260
602-948-6540

Canon U.S.A. Inc.
One Canon Plaza
Lake Success, NY 11042
516-488-6700

Colossal Graphics, Inc.
437 Emerson Street
Palo Alto, CA 94301
415-328-2264

Corel Systems Corp.
1600 Carling, Corel Building
Ottawa, Ontario Canada K1Z7M4
613-728-8200

Dicomed Corp.
1200 Portland Ave.
Minneapolis, MN 55440
612-885-3000

Digital Equipment Corp.
10 Tara Blvd.
Nashua, NH 03062-2802
603-884-5111

Eastman Kodak Company
343 State Street
Rochester, NY 14650
800-242-2424

Electronics For Imaging
2855 Campus Dr.
San Mateo, CA 94403
415-286-8600

Fractal Design Corp.
510 Lighthouse #5
Pacific Grove, CA 93950
408-655-8800

Fuji Photo Film U.S.A. Inc.
555 Taxter Rd.
Elmsford, NY 10523
800-FILM-FUJI

Hewlett-Packard
16399 West Bernardo Dr.
San Diego, CA 92127
619-487-4100

IBM Corp.
1133 Westchester Ave.
White Plains, NY 10604
800-431-2670

Ilford Imaging Systems
West 70 Century Rd.
Paramus, NJ 07653
201-265-6000

Imapro Corp.
2 Crosfield Ave., Ste. 208
West Nyack, NY 10994
914-353-4701

Intergraph Corp.
Huntsville, AL 35894-0001
800-826-3515

Island Graphics Corp.
4000 Civic Center Dr.
San Rafael, CA 94903
415-491-1000

Konica Business Machines
500 Day Hill Rd.
Windsor, CT 06095
203-683-2222

Letraset
40 Eisenhower Dr.
Paramus, NJ 07653
201-845-6100

Management Graphics, Inc.
1401 E. 79th St.
Minneapolis, MN 55425
612-854-1220

Media Cybernetics
8484 Georgia Ave., Ste. 200
Silver Spring, MD 20910
301-495-3305

Micrografx, Inc.
1303 E. Arapaho
Richardson, TX 75081
214-497-6431

Microsoft Corp.
One Microsoft Way
Redmond, WA 98052
206-882-8080

Microtek/U-Lead
680 Knox St.
Torrance, CA 90502
213-321-2121

Networked Picture Systems, Inc.
2953 Bunker Hill Ln. #202
Santa Clara, CA 95054
408-748-1677

Newer Technologies
7803 East Osie, #105
Wichita, KS 67207
316-685-4904

Nikon, Inc.
1300 Walt Whitman Rd.
Melville, NY 11747
516-547-4200

Novell, Inc.
122 East 1700 So.
Provo, UT 84601
800-453-1267

Pioneer Communications of America, Inc.
600 East Crescent Ave.
Upper Saddle River, NJ 07458
201-327-6400

Polaroid Corp.
549 Technology Square
Cambridge, MA 02139
617-577-2000

Radius, Inc.
1710 Fortune Dr.
San Jose, CA 95131
408-434-1010

RasterOps
2500 Walsh Ave.
Santa Clara, CA 95051
408-562-4200

Scitex America Corp.
8 Oak Park Drive
Bedford, MA 01730
617-275-5150

Silicon Graphics, Inc.
2011 North Shoreline Blvd.
P.O. Box 7311
Mountain View, CA 94039-7311

Sony Corporation of America
Sony Drive
Park Ridge, NJ 07656
201-930-1000

Stork Bedford B.V.
35 Wiggins Ave.
Bedford, MA 01730
617-275-9446

Sun Microsystems, Inc.
2550 Garcia Ave.
Mountain View, CA 94043
415-960-1300

SuperMac Technology
485 Potrero Ave.
Sunnyvale, CA 94086
408-245-2202

Superset, Inc.
3550 Dunhill St.
San Diego, CA 92121
619-452-8665

Tandy Corp.
1800 One Tandy Center
Fort Worth, TX 76102
817-390-3487

Toshiba Video Systems
82 Totowa Rd.
Wayne, NJ 07470
201-628-8000

U-Lead Systems
680 Knox St.
Torrance, CA 90502
213-321-2121

Ventura Software, Inc.
15175 Innovation Dr.
San Diego, CA 92128
800-822-8221

Xerox Corp.
Xerox Square
Rochester, NY 14644
716-423-5090

ZSoft Corp.
450 Franklin Road, Ste. 100
Marietta, GA 30067
404-428-0008

INDEX

A

Access
  announcement of   165
  software features   73–76
Adobe Photoshop   82
Advertising
  agency use of Photo CD
  applications of Photo CD   15, 51
Agfa   xii, **46**
Aldus Corp.   78
Aldus PageMaker   108
Apple Computer   13, 152, 168
Archiving
  with Photo CD   138
Authoring
  Portfolio discs   8

B

Base resolution. *See* Resolution
Books   17
Browser   77, **97**

C

Cachet   91
Calcomp   **69**
Calibration
  features of image editing software   81
  of monitors   54
Cameras
  35mm   1
  digital   10
  Kodak Instamatic   xii
Canon CLC 500   10, **64**

Carousel
    in PCD 5870   33
Case
    thumbnail images on   2
Catalog
    capacity of   9, 95
    format   24, **97–99**
Catalogs
    L.L. Bean   112
CD-I   6, 32, 135, 175
CD-ROM
    capacity of   12
    definition of   174
    drives   2
    multi-session drives   72
    standards   132–136
    writable   135
    XA   135
    XA drives   4
Chrominance   **26**, **42**
CIE   106
Clip art   121, 125
Color
    correction   81
    gamuts   **53**
    laser printers   **50**
    management   **52–57**, 91, 105
    models in Photoshop   83
    separations   83, 110
    spaces   104
    storing information   39
ColorSense   **53**, 165
ColorStudio   84
Compression
    JPEG   86
    of gamuts   **55**
    of Photo CD images   **41**
Computers
    applications of Photo CD   12

using Photo CD with   37
Consumer
      photography market   10
Copiers
      color   50, **65**
Copyright
      ownership of images   118–121
      Pro Photo CD format   126
Cropping
      in Access   75

D

Derivative works   120
Desktop publishing   13, **101**, 177
Device color profiles   **55**
DiceNet   **65**
Digital cameras
      DCS 200   10
Directories   96
Directory structure
      on Photo CD   160
Discs
      capacity of   5
      Portfolio   8
Drives
      magnetic   132
      multi-session   38
Dye sublimation printers. *See* Thermal dye transfer printers
Dynamic Data Exchange
      used in Access   75

E

George Eastman   xi
Eastman Kodak. *See* Kodak
EFI   **65**, 91
Encryption
      of images   37, 128

Exporting images
    from Access   74

F

Fiery controller   **65**
Film
    35mm frame size   25
    recorders   **67**
    transparencies   61
Formats
    Catalog   9
    for graphic files   **45**
    Medical   15
    of Photo CD   21
    Portfolio   8
    Pro Photo CD   33
Fuji Photo Film   **45**, 166

G

Gamma curve   81, 110
Gamuts
    color   **53**, 104

H

Halftoning   59
    screens in QuarkXPress   110
Halo Desktop Image   88
Hardware
    used in Photo CD   9
HDTV   74
    compatibility with Photo CD   xi
    suitability for 4Base images   **26**
Hertz
    technology   **63**
Home use   7
Huffman encoding   **42**

I

Image cropping
    in Access 75
Image editing 9
    features in software pack-
    ages 79
Image Pac
    definition of 180
    file sizes 27
    structure of 159
Image-In 89
Inkjet printers **62–63**
Intergraph 92
Interior design 158

J

Jewel case 5
JPEG 86, 181
Jukebox 139

K

Kiosks **70**, 127
    for trade shows 72
Kodak
    agreements with other ven-
    dors 13, 152
    CEO Kay Whitmore 157
    executives' views of Photo
    CD 154
Kodak Picture Ex-
    change 77, 141, **150–152**

L

Legal issues 122–125
Libraries
    for corporate images 90
Licensing
    Photo CD images 125

Litigation
  infringement cases   122
Lotus Development Corp.   153
Luminance   **26**, **42**

M

Macintosh
  support for Photo CD   73
Manuals   149
Manufacturing
  of Photo CD   **46**
Markets
  for Photo CD   16
Master
  format   **23**
Mastering
  workstations used   29
MCI   142
Medical
  applications of Photo CD   14
  format   24
  records on Photo CD   143
Microsoft   126
  Extensions for CD-ROM   135
Microsoft Windows. *See* Windows
Milestones
  in development of Photo CD   165
Model releases   124
Modems
  used with Kodak Picture Exchange   150
Multi-session
  drives   38
  recording   8
Multimedia
  applications of Portfolio   8
Museums
  use of Photo CD   **70**

N

Networking   148–149
Newspapers   **103**
NeXT Computer   92, 107

O

Offset lithography
    dots used in   61
OPI   109

P

Paint tools
    in image editing software   79
N.V. Philips   ix, 2
Photo albums   7, 11
Photo YCC   26
    as color standard   105
    color encoding   106
    converting from RGB   29
    device independence of   40
PhotoEdge   39, 76
PhotoFinish   87
PhotoStyler   84–86
Picture Publisher   86
Picture replacement   **102**
Players
    Kodak models   32
    laser imaging system   31
    using   4
    with Catalog format   **97**
Polaroid   xii, **46**
Portfolio   8, 24
    format   **99–101**
    resolution of   95
PostScript   **56**
    controller for large-format printers   **69**
Presentations
    using Photo CD   8, 157

using Portfolio **100**

Printers

    color laser   50

    large-format   **68**

    thermal wax   59

Printing and publishing

    applications of Photo CD   13

Prints

    from Photo CD   57

Professional Photo CD Library   138

Q

QuarkXPress   109–111

QuickTime   39

    support for Photo CD   73

R

Raster image processor   **56**

Renaissance   77

Resolution

    file sizes associated with   38

    levels on Photo CD disc   23, 26

    of Pro Photo CD   34

    of scanned images   115

    selecting the right image   113

    terminology in Access   74

RGB images   82

S

Sampling   188

Scan area

    of Photo CD   25

Scanners

    4045 film scanners   34

    calibration of   **54**

    desktop   **101**

    drum   116

    film   178

Kodak PCD Scanner   29
large-format   9
Photo CD   185
Security
    copyright protection   126
    features of Photo CD   36
    misuse of color copiers   71
Selection tools
    in image editing software   80
Shoebox   77, 151
Silver halide printers   **66**
Snapshot
    size image format   74
Software
    color management   91
    image enhancement   78–89
    Kodak products   6, 39, 73–78
    publishing packages   107–113
Sound
    in catalog format   **98**
    on Photo CD discs   **42**
    on Portfolio discs   **99**
SparcStation   30
Standards
    CD-ROM   132
    for Photo CD   136
    OPI   109
    prepress   **104–107**
Stock photos   123
Subsampling
    as compression method   **41**

T

Targets
    scanner   **55**
Television
    resolution of   26
    viewing images on   1, 7, 30

Thermal dye transfer printers   50, 60, 189
Thermal printers   59
J. Walter Thompson   15
Thumbnails
    images on case   3
    printed with index printer   30
    use for copyright registration   119
Transfer function   81

V

Ventura Publisher   111

W

Wallet
    size image format   74
Kay Whitmore   157
Windows   190
    DDE   75
    using Photo CD Access with   74
Workstations
    for mastering Photo CDs   29
    image enhancement   92
    Kodak professional imaging   35
Writing
    Kodak PCD Writer 200   141
    Kodak Writable CD   144
    of CD-ROMs   135

Z

ZSoft   87

PRODUCTION NOTE

This book was produced using a number of electronic publishing tools. All of the pages, including the halftone and color images, were produced electronically.

Several of the photographs in the book came from Photo CD. We used Kodak's Photo CD Access software running under Microsoft Windows to export the Photo CD images to TIFF format. Screen grabs from Windows were also saved in TIFF format. We then converted the IBM TIFF files to Macintosh format.

All images that did not come from Photo CD or were not computer-generated were scanned with a Hewlett-Packard Scanjet IIc or the Microtek ScanMaker 1850 slide scanner. We used Adobe Photoshop on the Macintosh to touch-up the scanned images.

Andrew Shalat designed the cover using Adobe Photoshop and Aldus Freehand on the Macintosh. We used Aldus PageMaker on the Macintosh to produce the page layout and generate the index.

We used Aldus PrePrint to produce color separations for the cover and the color insert. These pages were output directly to film using a Scitex Dolev imagesetter at RPI in Culver City, CA.

For the black-and-white pages, we used Aldus PressWise to produce impositions of our signatures directly from the

PostScript files generated by PageMaker. RPI used a Linotronic 530 imagesetter to output the signatures directly to negatives, with 16 pages per signature.

Delta Litho then imaged printing plates directly from the imposed signatures. The book was printed on a Mann press.

Digital Photography: Pictures of Tomorrow
by John Larish

This book from Micro Publishing Press is an applications-oriented guide targeted at computer users interested in digital photography and electronic imaging. It explains the basics of digital photography and the process of using digital images in computer-generated publications. Numerous case studies show how users in various industries are already putting digital photography to work.

Whether you're an amateur photographer, desktop publisher, multimedia producer, or electronics hobbyist, you'll find this book to be a valuable resource.

Key Topics

- Capturing and Storing Photographs
- Processing Images
- Creating Pages
- Producing Soft and Hard Copy
- Multimedia Applications

The Author
John Larish is the editor of *Electronic Photography News* and a former senior marketing staff member at Eastman Kodak Company.

ORDER FORM

Please send ____ copies of *Digital Photography: Pictures of Tomorrow*

❑ Enclosed is my check for $27.95 plus $3 shipping. (California residents add 8.25% sales tax.)

❑ Please charge my q MasterCard q Visa q American Express

Number _____ Exp Date _____

Signature _____

Name _____

Company _____

Address _____

City _____ State _____ Zip _____

Telephone _____

Remit to: Micro Publishing Press, 21150 Hawthorne Blvd. #104, Torrance, CA 90503 (310) 371-5787 Fax:(310) 542-0849